# THE GREEK GODS

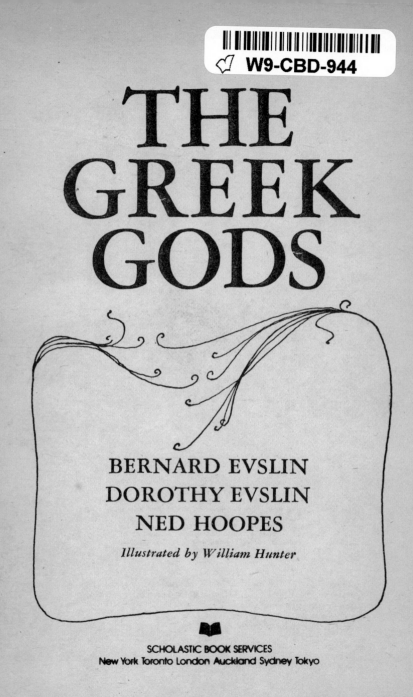

**BERNARD EVSLIN**
**DOROTHY EVSLIN**
**NED HOOPES**

*Illustrated by William Hunter*

SCHOLASTIC BOOK SERVICES
New York Toronto London Auckland Sydney Tokyo

32 31 30 29 28 27 26 25 24 23 22                    2 3 4 5/8
                    Printed in the U.S.A.                    11

# CONTENTS

the Pantheon

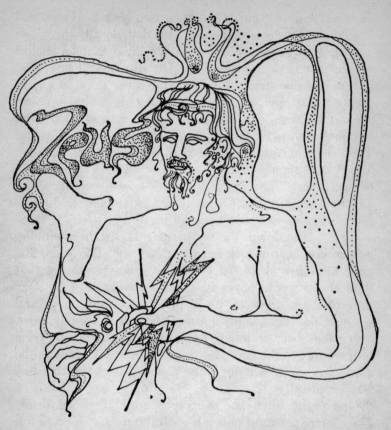

Cronos, father of the gods, who gave his name to time, married his sister Rhea, goddess of earth. Now, Cronos had become king of the gods by killing his father Oranos, the First One, and the dying Oranos had prophesied, saying, "You murder me now, and steal my throne — but one of your own sons will dethrone you, for crime begets crime."

So Cronos was very careful. One by one, he swallowed his children as they were born: First, three daughters —

Hestia, Demeter, and Hera; then two sons — Hades and Poseidon. One by one, he swallowed them all.

Rhea was furious. She was determined that he should not eat her next child who she felt sure would be a son. When her time came, she crept down the slope of Olympus to a dark place to have her baby. It was a son, and she named him Zeus. She hung a golden cradle from the branches of an olive tree, and put him to sleep there. Then she went back to the top of the mountain. She took a rock and wrapped it in swaddling clothes and held it to her breast, humming a lullaby. Cronos came snorting and bellowing out of his great bed, snatched the bundle from her, and swallowed it, clothes and all.

Rhea stole down the mountainside to the swinging golden cradle, and took her son down into the fields. She gave him to a shepherd family to raise, promising that their sheep would never be eaten by wolves.

Here Zeus grew to be a beautiful young boy, and Cronos, his father, knew nothing about him. Finally, however, Rhea became lonely for him and brought him back to the court of the gods, introducing him to Cronos as the new cupbearer. Cronos was pleased because the boy was beautiful.

One night Rhea and Zeus prepared a special drink. They mixed mustard and salt with the nectar. Next morning, after a mighty swallow, Cronos vomited up first a stone, and then Hestia, Demeter, Hera, Hades, and Poseidon — who, being gods, were still undigested, still alive. They thanked Zeus, and immediately chose him to be their leader.

Then a mighty battle raged. Cronos was joined by the Titans, his half-brothers, huge, twisted, dark creatures taller than trees, whom he kept pent up in the mountains until there was fighting to be done. They attacked the young gods furiously. But Zeus had allies too. He had gone to darker caverns — caves under caves under caves, deep in the mountainside — formed by the first bubbles of the cooling earth. Here, Cronos, thousands of centuries before (a short time in the life of a god) had pent up other monsters, the one-eyed Cyclopes, and the Hundred-handed Ones. Zeus unshackled these ugly cousins and led them against the Titans.

There was a great rushing and tumult in the skies. The people on earth heard mighty thunder, and saw mountains shatter. The earth quaked and tidal waves rolled as the gods fought. The Titans were tall as trees, and old Cronos was a crafty leader. He attacked fiercely, driving the young gods before him. But Zeus had laid a trap. Halfway up the slope of Olympus, he whistled for his cousins, the Hundred-handed Ones, who had been lying in ambush. They took up huge boulders, a hundred each, and hurled them downhill at the Titans. The Titans thought the mountain itself was falling on them. They broke ranks, and fled.

The young goat-god Pan was shouting with joy. Later he said that it was his shout that made the Titans flee. That is where we get the word "panic."

Now the young gods climbed to Olympus, took over the castle, and Zeus became their king. No one knows what happened to Cronos and his Titans. But sometimes mountains still explode in fire, and the earth still quakes, and no one knows exactly why.

One story says that Zeus killed Cronos with a scythe — the same one that Cronos had used on Oranos. Perhaps this is the real meaning behind the greeting-card pictures we exchange on New Year's Day, a rosy little baby confronting an old man who carries a scythe. Memories of the old gods crop up in odd places.

Now these gods reigned for some three thousand years. There were many of them, but twelve chief ones. Zeus married his sister Hera — a family habit. They were always quarreling. He angered her by his infidelities; she enraged him with her strategies. She was the queen of intriguers, and always found it easy to outwit Zeus who was busy with many things.

Once, she persuaded the other gods into a plot against him. She drugged his drink; they surrounded him as he slept, and bound him with rawhide thongs. He raged and roared and swore to destroy them, but they had stolen his thunderbolt, and he could not break the thongs.

But his faithful cousin, the Hundred-handed Briareus, who had helped him against the Titans, was working as his gardener. He heard the quarreling under the palace window, looked in, and saw his master bound to the couch. He reached through with his hundred long arms, and unbound the hundred knots.

Zeus jumped from the couch and seized his thunderbolt. The terrified plotters fell to their knees, weeping and pleading. He seized Hera and hung her in the sky, binding her with golden chains. And the others did not dare to rescue her, although her voice was like the wind sobbing. But her weeping kept Zeus awake. In the morning he said he would free her if she swore never to rebel again. She promised, and Zeus promised to mend his ways too. But they kept watching each other.

Zeus was king of the gods, lord of the sky. His sister Demeter was the earth-goddess, lady of growing things. His sister Hera was also his wife, queen of the gods. His brother Poseidon, was god of the sea. His other brother, Hades, ruled a dark domain, the underworld, the land beyond death.

The other gods in the Pantheon were Zeus's children; three of them were also Hera's. These were Ares, the god of war; Hephaestus, the smith-god, forger of weapons; and Eris, goddess of discord, who shrieks beside Ares in his battle chariot. The rest of Zeus's children were born out of wedlock. Three of them entered the Pantheon.

The first was Athene, and the story of how she was born is told in the next chapter.

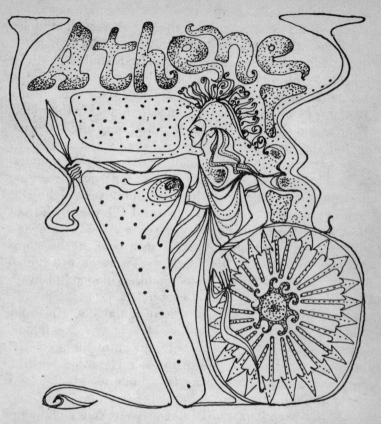

Athene

Zeus was strolling on Olympus one morning, and noticed a new maiden walking in his garden. She was Metis, a Titaness, daughter of one of his old enemies. But the war was long ago, and she was beautiful. He charged down the slope after her.

She turned into a hawk and flew away. He turned into a hawk and flew after. She flew over the lake and dived in and became a fish. He became a fish and swam after her. She climbed on the bank, and became a serpent and wriggled away. He changed himself into a serpent, and wriggled after, and caught her.

After he left her, he heard a bird cry and a fish leap, and those wild sounds combined to become a prophecy, which the rattling leaves echoed. "Oh, Zeus, Metis will bear a child, a girl child. But if she bears again, it will be a son who will depose you as you deposed Cronos."

The next day Zeus walked in his garden again, and found Metis there. This time she did not flee. He spoke softly to her, and smiled. She came to him. Suddenly, he opened his mouth and swallowed her.

That afternoon he suffered a headache — the worst headache that anyone, god or mortal, had suffered since the beginning of time. It was exactly as if someone were inside him with a spear, thrusting at all the soft places in his head. He shouted for Hephaestus, who came rushing up with hammer and wedge. Zeus put his head on the anvil, and Hephaestus split the mighty skull; then he leaped back, frightened, because out of the head sprang a tall maiden in armor, holding a long spear.

This was Athene, the gray-eyed, the wide-browed. The manner of her birth gave her domain over intellectual activities. It was she who taught man how to use tools. She taught him to invent the ax, the plough, the ox-yoke, the wheel, and the sail. She taught his wife to spin and weave. She concocted the science of numbers and taught it to man — but never to woman. She hated Ares, and took great pleasure in thwarting him on the field of battle. For all his mighty strength, she often beat him, because she was a mistress of strategy. Before battle, captains prayed to her for tactics. Before trial, judges prayed to her for wisdom. It was she who stated that compassion was the best part of wisdom. The other gods didn't know what she meant by this. But some men understood, and were grateful. All in all, she was perhaps the best-loved god in the Pantheon; the people of Athens named their beautiful city after her.

There are many stories about Athene — about her skill in battle, her wisdom, and her kindliness. But, like the other gods, she was also very jealous. One of the best stories is that of Arachne.

Arachne was a young girl who lived in Lydia, famous for its purple dye. Her joy was weaving, and she wove the most beautiful things anyone had ever seen: cloaks so light you could not feel them about your shoulders, but warmer than fur; tapestries wrought with pictures so marvelous that birds would fly through the window and try to eat the cherries off the woven bough. She was a very young girl, and everyone praised her — and soon she began to praise herself. She said:

"I, I am the greatest weaver in all the world. The greatest since the world began, no doubt. In fact, I can weave better than Athene herself."

Athene heard this, of course. The gods are very quick to hear criticism, and very swift to act. So she came to earth, to the little village where Arachne lived.

The girl was inside, spinning. She heard a knock at the door, and opened it. There stood a lady so tall, so sternly beautiful that Arachne knew she must be a goddess, and she was afraid she knew which one. She fell on her knees. Far above her head she heard a voice speaking softly, saying terrible things.

"Yes, miserable girl, I am Athene. I am the goddess you have mocked. Is there any reason I should not kill you?"

Arachne shook her head, weeping. She could not answer.

"Very well," said Athene. "Prepare yourself for death. You have defied the gods, and must die."

Then Arachne stood up and said, "Before I die, great Athene, let me give you a present." She went in and took a lovely cloak she had woven, and gave it to her. And said: "Take this cloak. It must often get cold up high on Olympus. This will shield you from the wind. Please take it. I am sure you have nothing so fine."

Athene shook her head and said, "Poor child. You are being destroyed by your own worth. Your talent has poisoned you with pride like the sting of a scorpion. So that which makes beauty brings death. But it is a handsome cloak, and I appreciate the gift. I will give you one chance. You have boasted that you can spin and weave better than I . . . than I, who invented the loom and the spinning wheel, the distaff and the spindle, and out of the fleece of the clouds wove the first counterpane for my father, Zeus, who likes to sleep warm, and dyed it with the colors of the sunset. But you say you can weave better than I. Very well, you shall have a chance to prove it. And your own villagers shall judge. Seven days from today, we shall meet. You will set your spinning wheel in that meadow, and I shall be in my place, and we shall have a contest. You will weave what you will, and I shall do so too. Then we will show what we have done, and the people will judge. If you win, I shall withdraw the punishment. If you lose, it is your life. Do you agree?"

"Oh, yes," said Arachne. "Thank you, dear godde⁄ sparing my life."

"It is not yet spared," said Athene.

The word flashed from village to village. ⁄ time came, not only Arachne's neighbors, but⁄ ple in the land had gathered in the great me⁄

the contest. Arachne's house was the last in the village, and faced the great meadow. She had set up her loom outside the door. Athene sat on a low flat hill overlooking the field. Her loom was as large as Arachne's cottage.

The girl went first. At the sight of her sitting spinning there in the sunlight, the crowd pushed in so close she hardly had room to work. Her white hands danced among the flax, and she worked so quickly, so deftly, that she seemed to have forgotten the loom, and to be weaving in the air. Swiftly and more swiftly she tapped on the wool with her fingers, making it billow and curl, then rolling it quickly into a ball, then shaking it out again, straining the wool into long shining threads with quick little pokes of her thumb at her spindle. It was said that her working was as beautiful as her work, and when she was told that, she always smiled and said, "It is the same thing." So she wove, and the people watched. Then the finished cloth began to come from the loom, and everybody laughed to see. For they were joyous scenes. Morning scenes: a little boy and a little girl running in a green field among yellow flowers, chased by a black dog; a maiden at a window dreamily combing her hair; a young man watching the sea, counting the waves. And, later, in a purple dusk, that same young man and girl standing under a tree looking at each other. Swiftly and more swiftly the white hands danced between loom and spindle. She wove bouquets of flowers for the wedding, and a wedding gown for the bride, and a gorgeous cloak for the young husband. And, remembering what Athene had said before, she spun a counterpane for their bed. Each square not a block of color, but a little picture — one from the childhood of the man, one from the childhood of the bride, all together, ing, as their memories would mix now.

THE GREEK GODS: THE PANTHEON

The counterpane was last. When she arose and snapped it out, the people gasped and laughed and wept with joy. And Arachne curtsied toward the low hill, and Athene began to spin.

The goddess had conjured up a flock of plump white woolly clouds about her hilltop. So she did not have to comb fleece or draw thread; she used cloud-wool, the finest stuff in all the world. And she dyed it with the colors of the dawn, and the colors of the sunset, and the colors of sleep, and the colors of storm. Now the whole western part of the sky was her loom. She flung great tapestries across the horizon. Scenes from Olympus — things that mortal man had never hoped to see. Almost too terrible to see . . . Cronos cutting up Oranos with a scythe . . . Zeus charging across the firmament with his Hundred-handed Ones, shattering the Titans . . . the binding of Zeus, the punishment of Hera. Zeus chasing Metis as hawk and fish and snake. Then the birth of Athene herself, springing from Zeus's broken head. Then, more quiet scenes. Athene teaching the arts to man. Teaching him to plough, to sail, to ride in chariots; teaching the women to spin. And, then, finally — muddling it all up, poking her long spindle among the woven clouds and mixing them and stirring up a dark strange picture — the future of man. Man growing huge and monstrous, his trees turning to spikes, his fields to stone. Swollen and dropsical with pride, building something so loathsome he had to look away while he was making it.

This was too much for the multitude. The vast crowd fell on its knees and wept. Arachne was watching. She had never moved from the time Athene had started to work, but stood there straight with pale face and glittering eyes, watching. And when the people fell on their knees, she turned and went away. She walked quietly to a grove of trees and there took a rope and hanged herself.

Athene came down from the hill, and spoke no word to the people, who dispersed. Then she went to the grove and saw Arachne hanging there. The girl's face was black, her eyes were bulging, her hair was streaming. Athene reached her long arm and touched the girl on the shoulder. The face grew blacker, and the eyes bulged more. The body shrank; the arms and legs dwindled and multiplied. Then Athene touched the rope. It shriveled, growing thinner and thinner, until it was a frail shining strand. And there at the end of this shining silken hair swung a small hairy creature with many legs.

It looked at Athene, then turned and scuttled up its thread, drawing it up as it climbed. It floated away over the grass until it came to a low bush, and cast another loop, and sat there practicing, for it knew that now it was meant to spin without rivalry until the end of time.

That is why spiders are called Arachnids by those who know them best.

After Cronos was deposed, the three sons threw dice for his empire. Zeus, the youngest, won — and chose the sky. Poseidon smiled to himself because the sky was empty, and he knew that the impulsive Zeus had chosen it because it looked so high. And now, he, Poseidon, could choose as he would have done if he had won. He chose the sea. He had always wanted it; it is the best place for adventures and secrets, and makes claim on land and sky. Hades, who was always unlucky, had to take the underworld. The earth was held as a commonwealth, and left to the goddesses to manage.

Poseidon left Olympus and came to his kingdom. He immediately set about building a huge underwater palace with a great pearl and coral throne. He needed a queen, and chose Thetis, a beautiful Nereid, or water nymph. But it was prophesied that any son born to Thetis would be greater than his father, so Poseidon decided to try elsewhere. (The prophecy came true. The son of Thetis was Achilles, who undoubtedly was greater than his father Peleus.)

Poseidon chose another Nereid named Amphitrite. But like his brother Zeus, he was a great traveler, and had hundreds of children in different places. He was a very difficult god, changeful and quarrelsome. Although he did bear grudges, he could be pleased, and then his smile was radiant. He liked jokes, and thought up very curious forms for his creatures. He liked to startle nymphs with monsters, and concocted the octopus, the squid, the sea-polyp or jellyfish, the swordfish, blowfish, sea cow, and many others. Once, trying to appease Amphitrite's jealous rage, he thought up the dolphin, and gave it to her as a gift.

He was greedy and aggressive, always trying to add to his kingdom. Once, he claimed Attica as his own, and stabbed his trident into the hillside where the Acropolis still stands, and a spring of salt water spouted. Now the people of Athens did not want to belong to the kingdom of the sea. They were afraid of Poseidon, who had a habit of seizing all the youth of a town when he was in the mood. So they prayed to be put under the protection of another god. Athene heard their prayers. She came down and planted an olive tree by the side of the spring. Poseidon was enraged. His face darkened and he roared with fury, raising a storm. A fishing fleet was blown off the sea and never came to port. He challenged Athene to single combat, and threatened to stir up a tidal wave to break over the city if she refused. She accepted. Zeus heard the sound of this quarreling. He came down and decreed a truce. Then all the gods sat in council to hear the rival claims. After hearing both Athene and Poseidon, they voted to award the city to Athene because her olive tree was the better gift. After that, Athenians had to be very careful when they went to sea, and were often unfortunate in their naval battles.

Poseidon was very fond of Demeter, and pursued her hotly whenever he thought about it. He cornered her, finally, one hot afternoon in a mountain pass, and demanded that she love him. She didn't know what to do — he was so huge, so implacable, so persistent.

Finally, Demeter said, "Give me a gift. You have made creatures for the sea; now make me a land animal. But a beautiful one, the most beautiful ever seen."

She thought she was safe, because she believed he could make only monsters. She was amazed when he made her a horse, and gasped with delight when she saw it. And Poseidon was so struck by his handiwork that he swiftly made a herd of horses that began to gallop about the meadow, tossing their heads, flirting their tails, kicking up their back legs, and neighing joyously. And he was so fascinated by the horses that he forgot all about Demeter, and leaped on one and rode off. Later, he made another herd of green ones for his undersea stables. But Demeter kept the first herd; from that all the horses in the world have descended.

Another story says it took Poseidon a full week to make the horse. During that time he made and cast aside many other creatures that didn't come out right. But he simply threw them away without killing them, and they made their way into the world. From them have come the camel, the hippopotamus, the giraffe, the donkey, and the zebra.

In another story, Demeter turned herself into a mare to escape Poseidon. But he immediately changed himself into a stallion, galloped after her and caught her. From this courtship came a wild horse, Arion, and the nymph named Despoena.

Demeter was also a moon goddess. And all through mythology there is a connection between horse and moon and sea. The she-horse is given a sea-name,"mare"; the moon swings the tides, the waves have white manes, the dripping horses stamp on the beach, and their hooves leave moon-shaped marks. An old, old thing that has not entirely disappeared.

When the Greeks buried their dead, they put a coin under the corpse's tongue so his soul could pay the fare on the ferry that crossed the river Styx. It was Charon who rowed the boat; he was a miser. Souls who couldn't pay for the ride had to wait on this side of the river. Sometimes they came back to haunt those who hadn't given them the fare.

On the other side of the river was a great wall. Its gate was guarded by Cerberus, a three-headed dog who had an appetite for live meat and attacked everyone but spirits.

Beyond the gate, in Tartarus, was a great wide field shaded by black poplars. Here lived the dead — heroes and cowards, soldiers, shepherds, priests, minstrels, slaves. They wandered back and forth aimlessly. When they spoke they twittered like bats. Here they awaited trial by three judges — Minos, Rhadamanthys, and Aeacus.

Those who had particularly displeased the gods were given special punishment. Sisyphus, an avaricious king of Corinth, must always push a huge rock uphill. Each time he gets it halfway up, it breaks loose and rolls down to the bottom, and he must begin again. And this he will do for all time. Tantalus who had committed a sin has been given a burning thirst, and set chin-deep in a cool, clear stream of water. But every time he bends to put his lips to the water, it shrinks away, and he can never drink. Here he will stand as long as Sisyphus rolls his stone.

But these are special cases. Most of the souls were judged to be not too good and not too bad, but simply dead. They went back to the field, which is called the Field of Asphodel, to wait — for nothing.

Those judged to be of unusual virtue went to the Elysian Fields close by. Here it was always holiday. The air was full of music. The shades danced and played all day long — all night long too, for the dead need no sleep. Also, these happy spirits had the option of being reborn on earth. Only the bravest accepted. There was a special part of Elysium called the Isles of the Blest. Here lived those who had been three times born, and three times gained Elysium.

Hades and his queen lived in a great palace made of black rock. He was very jealous of his brothers, and scarcely ever left his domain. He was fiercely possessive, gloated over every new arrival, and demanded a headcount from Charon at the close of each day. Never did he allow any of his subjects to escape. Nor did he allow a mortal to visit Tartarus, and return. There were only two exceptions to this rule, and those are other stories.

The palace grounds and the surrounding fields were called Erebos; this was the deepest part of the underworld. No birds flew here, but the sound of wings was heard; for here lived the Erinyes, or Furies, who were older than the gods. Their names were Tisiphone, Alecto, and Megaera. They were hags, with snaky hair, red-hot eyes, and yellow teeth. They slashed the air with metal-studded whips, and when they found a victim, they whipped the flesh from his bones. Their task was to visit earth and punish evil-doers, especially those who had escaped other punishment. They were greatly feared; no one dared say their name. But they were referred to as the "Eumenides," or Kindly Ones. Hades valued them. They enriched his kingdom, for their attentions persuaded people to suicide. He enjoyed their conversation. When they returned to Erebus after their work was done, they circled low over the palace grounds, screaming their tale, and the latest gossip.

Hades was well-cast to rule the dead. He was violent, loathed change, and was given to slow black rage. His most dramatic hour was when he kidnaped Persephone and made her his queen. But that belongs to the next story.

Demeter means "Barley-mother." Another name for her is Ceres, from which we get the word "cereal." She was the goddess of the cornfield, mistress of planting and harvesting, lady of growing things. Zeus was very fond of her. He always obliged her with rain when her fields were thirsty. He gave her two children, a boy and a girl. The girl was named Persephone, and Demeter loved her very much.

Persephone was raised among flowers and looked like

a flower herself. Her body was as pliant as a stem, her skin soft as petals, and she had pansy eyes. She took charge of flowers for her mother. She was adept at making up new kinds and naming them.

One day she went farther than usual — across a stream, through a grove of trees, to a little glade. She carried her paintpot, for she had seen a stand of tall waxy lilies she had decided to stripe. As she was painting their faces, she saw a bush she hadn't noticed before. She went to look at it. It was a very strange bush, with thick, green, glossy leaves, and hung with large red berries that trembled on their stems like drops of blood. She stared at the bush. She didn't know whether she liked it or not. She decided she did not, and seized it by its branches, and pulled. But it was toughly rooted and hard to pull. She was used to getting her own way. She set herself and gave a mighty tug. Up came the bush; its long roots dragged out of the ground, leaving a big hole. She tossed the bush aside, and turned to go back to her lilies, but she heard a rumbling sound and turned back. The noise that grew louder and louder was coming from the hole. To her horror, the hole seemed to be spreading, opening like a mouth, and the rumbling grew to a jangling, crashing din.

Out of the hole leaped six black horses, dragging behind them a golden chariot. In the chariot stood a tall figure in a flowing black cape. On his head was a black crown. She had no time to scream. He reached out his long arm, snatched her into the chariot, and lashed his horses. They curvetted in the air, and plunged into the hole again. When they had gone, the hole closed.

Demeter was frantic when the girl didn't come home, and rushed out to search for her. The tall green-clad goddess rode in a light wicker chariot behind a swift white horse, a gift from Poseidon. She sped here and there, calling, "Persephone . . . Persephone. . . ." But no one answered. All night long she searched, and, as dawn broke, she came to the glade. There she saw the uprooted bush and the trampled grass. She leaped from her chariot. Then she saw something that stabbed her through — Persephone's little paintpot, overturned. She lifted her head to the sky and howled like a she-wolf. Then she fell still, and listened. The sun was rising; the birds had begun to gossip. They told each other of the heedless girl, and the strange bush, and the hole, and the chariot, and the black rider, and how surprised the girl was when he caught her.

Then Demeter spoke softly, questioning the birds. They told her enough for her to know who had taken her daughter. She put her face in her hands and wept. Just then a little boy came running into the meadow to pick some flowers. When he saw Demeter, he laughed. He had never seen a grownup crying before. But when she looked up, he stopped laughing. She pointed at him, whispering, and he was immediately changed into a lizard. But he hadn't learned to scuttle yet, and just sat there looking at Demeter a moment too long, for a hawk swooped and caught him. He was a lizard for only a short while.

Demeter climbed back into her chariot and sped to Olympus. She charged into the throne room where Zeus sat.

"Justice!" she cried. "Justice! . . . Your brother Hades has stolen my daughter — *our* daughter."

"Peace, good sister," said Zeus. "Compose yourself. Hades' courtship has been a trifle abrupt, perhaps, but after all he is my brother — *our* brother — and is accounted a good match. Think, sweet Demeter. It is difficult for our daughter to look beyond the family without marrying far beneath her."

"Never!" cried Demeter. "It must not be! Anyone but Hades! Don't you realize this is a spring child, a flower child, a delicate unopened bud. No ray of sunlight ever pierces that dank hole he calls his kingdom. She'll wither and die."

"She is our daughter," said Zeus. "I fancy she has a talent for survival. Pray, think it over."

Then Demeter noticed that Zeus was holding a new thunderbolt, a marvelously wrought zigzag lance of lightning, volt-blue, radiant with energy. And she realized that Hades, who in his deep realms held all stores of silver and gold, had sent Zeus a special gift. It would be difficult to obtain justice.

"Once again," she said, "will you restore my daughter to me?"

"My dear," said Zeus, "when your rage cools, you will realize that this is a fine match, the very best thing for the child. Please, go back to earth and give yourself a chance to be intelligent about this."

"I will go back to earth," said Demeter, "and I will not return until you send for me."

Weeks passed. Then Zeus found his sleep being disturbed by sounds of lamentation. He looked down upon the earth, and saw a grievous sight. Nothing grew. The fields were blasted and parched. Trees were stripped of leaves, standing blighted, with the blazing sun beating down. The soil was hard and cracked, covered with the shriveled brown husks of wheat and corn and barley killed in the bud. And there was no green place anywhere. The people were starving. The cattle had nothing to eat; the game could find nothing and had fled. And a great wailing and lamentation arose as the people lifted their faces to Olympus and prayed for Zeus to help them.

"Well," he thought to himself, fingering his new thunderbolt, "I suppose we shall have to compromise."

He sent for Demeter. When she came, he said, "I have been thinking. Perhaps I have not been quite fair to you."

"No," said Demeter.

"Do you still wish your daughter's return?"

"Yes," said Demeter. "While she is gone, no crops will grow. No tree will bear, no grass will spring. While she is gone and while I mourn, the earth will grow as dry and shriveled as my heart, and will put forth no green thing."

"Very well," said Zeus. "In light of all the facts, this is my judgment. Your daughter shall be restored to you, and shall remain with you. However, if any food has passed her lips during her sojourn in Tartarus, then she must remain there. This is the law of abode, older than our decrees, and even I am powerless to revoke it."

"She will have been too sad to eat," cried Demeter. "No food will have passed her lips. She shall return to me and remain with me. You have spoken, and I hold you to your word."

Zeus whistled, and Hermes, the messenger god, appeared. Zeus sent him with a message to Hades demanding Persephone's release.

"Will you ride with me to the gates of Tartarus?" cried Demeter. "I have the swiftest horse in the world, given me by Poseidon."

"Thank you, good aunt," said Hermes. "But I believe my winged shoes are even faster."

And he flew out of the window.

In the meantime, Persephone was in Erebos with the dark king. After the first few days of haste and brutality and strangeness, he began to treat her very gently, and with great kindness. He gave her rubies and diamonds to play jacks with, had dresses spun for her of gold and silver thread, ordered her a throne of the finest ebony, and gave her a crown of black pearls. But she made herself very difficult to please. She tossed her head, stamped her foot, and turned from him. She would not speak to him, and said she would never forgive him. She said she wanted to go home to her mother, and that she had to attend to her flowers, and that she hated him and always would. As she launched these tirades at him, he would stand and listen and frown, and keep listening until she flounced away. Then he would go and get her another gift.

Secretly, though, so secretly that she didn't even tell it to herself, she was rather enjoying the change. She did miss the sunshine and the flowers, but there was much to amuse her. Secretly she gloated upon her power over this most fearsome monarch. Secretly, she enjoyed his gifts and his efforts to please her . . . and marveled at the way he was obeyed. Although she never forgot how he had frightened her when he came charging out of that hole in his chariot, she admired the lofty set of his black-robed figure, the majestic shoulders, the great impatient hands, and his gloomy black eyes. But she knew that part of her power over him was disdain, and so kept flouting and abusing him, and, which made him gloomier than ever, refused to let a crumb of food pass her lips.

He tried every way he knew to tempt her into eating. His cook prepared the most delicious meals and his servants bore them to her chamber. But she would pretend not to notice a thing, and sit there holding her head high, not even allowing her nostrils to twitch, although the rich smells were making her wild with hunger. She swore she would not eat a mouthful until he had returned her to her mother.

He was desperate to please her. He set aside a corner of the palace grounds for a dark garden, and gave her rare seeds to plant — magical blooms that did not need the sunlight. She grew a species of black orchid, and mushrooms, and nightshade, henbane, and hellebore. He gave her a little boy to help her garden, a very clever little gardener, a new spirit. He was very deft, and good company too, although she noticed that his eyes were a bit lidless. She had no way of knowing that he was the same little boy her mother had turned into a lizard and fed to a hawk. But he knew who she was.

She had other amusements too. She liked to wander in the Elysian Fields and dance with the happy shades. She was fascinated by the torments, particularly the funny man trying to roll the stone uphill, and always having to start over again. She pitied Tantalus, and when no one was looking, cupped some water in her hands and gave it to him to drink. And he thanked her in a deep sad voice. But after she left, it was worse than ever; he knew she would not remember him again, and this one flash of hope made the ordeal worse.

Still, she liked her garden best, and that was where she spent most of her time — more time than ever, because she was so hungry she didn't know what to do, and she didn't want Hades to see how she felt. She knew he would think up more delicious things to tempt her if he thought she was weakening.

Standing in the garden one afternoon, half-hidden in a clump of nightshade, she saw the little boy eating something. It was a red fruit, and he was eating it juicily. He saw her watching and came toward her smiling, his mouth stained with red juice. He held out his hand. It was a pomegranate, her favorite fruit.

"We're alone," he whispered. "No one will see you. No one will know. Quickly now — eat!"

She looked about. It was true. No one could see them. She felt her hands acting by themselves, as though she had nothing to do with them. She watched as the fingers curled savagely and ripped the fruit across. They dug in, plucked out seeds, and offered them to her lips. One . . . two . . . three . . . she thought she had never tasted anything so delicious as these tiny tart juicy seeds. Just as she swallowed her sixth seed, a high glad yelling cry split the air, and the pomegranate dropped to the ground. It was a cry that any god recognized — Hermes' keen herald shout, meaning that he was coming with news, good or bad, but worthy of high attention.

She raced to the palace. The little gardener scooped up the pomegranate and raced after her. Sure enough, it was cousin Hermes, his hair tumbled from the wind, the wings on his feet still fluttering from the speed of his going.

"Good day, cousin," he said.

Hades loomed next to him, scowling blackly.

"I bring you a message from your mother. She wants you home. And your host has kindly agreed to an early departure. How are you? Haven't eaten anything here, I hope. No? Good! Let's be on our way."

He put his arm around her waist, and they rose in the air. And Persephone, looking back, saw the little gardener rush to Hades with the pomegranate in his hand.

By the time Persephone had come home to her mother, Hades had already been to Olympus, and had presented his case to Zeus. Zeus pronouncd his judgment. Because the girl had eaten six seeds of the pomegranate she would have to spend six months with Hades each year.

"Never mind, Mother," said Persephone. "Don't cry. We must be happy for the time that I am here."

"I suffer!" cried Demeter. "I suffer! Here . . ." She struck herself on the chest. "Here — in my mother's heart. And if I suffer, then everyone else shall suffer too. For the months that you spend with that scoundrel, no grass will grow, no flowers blow, no trees will bear. So long as you are below, there will be desolation everywhere."

That is why summer and winter are the way they are. That is why there is a time for planting, and a time when the earth must sleep under frost.

# BIRTH OF THE TWINS

Zeus pursued a nymph named Leto. But Hera was watching, so he changed Leto into a quail, and then himself into a quail, and they met in a glade. Here the sun sifted through the trees and striped the grass with shadows, and it was difficult to see two quail whose feathers were brown and lighter brown. But the eyes of jealousy are very sharp, and Hera saw them. She flung a curse, saying, "Leto, you will grow heavy with child, but you shall not bear anywhere the sun shines."

She sent the great serpent, Python, to enforce her curse, to hunt Leto out of any sunny place she might try to rest. Zeus sent the south wind to help the girl, and she was carried on the wings of the warm strong wind to an island called Delos. Python swam after. Before he could reach the island, however, Zeus unmoored it and sent it floating swiftly away, pushed by the south wind, more swiftly than Python could swim. Here, on this lovely island, Leto gave birth to twins — Artemis and Apollo.

Artemis

Father Zeus was by no means an attentive parent. He had so many children in so many different circumstances he could scarcely keep them all in mind. However, he was not permitted to forget Leto's children. They were too beautiful. And beauty was the quality he found most attractive. As he looked down from Olympus, their faces seemed to blaze from among all the children on earth. It seemed to him that they cast their own light, these twins, each one different — Apollo a ruddy light, Artemis a silver light. And he knew that they were true godlings and must be brought to Olympus.

He sent for them on their third birthday. He had Hephaestus make Apollo a golden bow and a quiver of golden arrows that could never be emptied, and a golden chariot drawn by golden ponies. But he withheld Artemis' gifts; he preferred her, and he wanted her to ask him for things. He took her on his lap, and said, "And what gifts would you fancy, little maid?"

She said, "I wish to be your maiden always, never a woman. And I want many names in case I get bored with one. I want a bow and arrow too — but silver, not gold. I want an embroidered deerskin tunic short enough to run in. I need fifty ocean nymphs to sing for me, and twenty wood nymphs to hunt with me. And I want a pack of hounds, please — fierce, swift ones. I want the mountains for my special places, and one city. One will be enough; I don't like cities." She reached up and played with his beard, and smiled at him. "Yes? May I have all these things? May I?"

Zeus answered, "For a child like you it is worthwhile braving Hera's wrath once in a while. You shall have more than you ask for. You shall have the gift of eternal chastity, and also the gift of changing your mind about it at any time, which will help you not to want to. And, finally, the greatest gift of all: You shall go out and choose your own gifts so that they will have a special value."

She kissed him, and whispered her thanks into his ear, and then went running off to choose her gifts. She went to the woods and to the river and to the ocean stream and selected the most beautiful nymphs for her court. She visited Hephaestus in his smoking smithy inside the mountain, and said, "I've come for my bow. A silver one, please."

He said, "Silver is more difficult to work than gold. It needs cool light; it should be made underwater. You must go deep beneath the sea, off the island of Lipara, where my Cyclopes are making a horse trough for Poseidon, who thinks of nothing but horses these days."

So Artemis and her nymphs swam underwater to where the Cyclopes were hammering at a great trough. The nymphs were frightened at the sight of the huge one-eyed scowling brutes, and they hated the noise of the hammering. But Artemis jumped up on the forge and said, "I come with a message from Hephaestus. He bids you put aside this horse trough and make me a silver bow and a quiver of silver arrows which will fill again as soon as it is empty. If you do this I shall give you the first game I shoot." The Cyclopes, who were very greedy and tired of working on the horse trough, agreed.

When they had finished her bow, she thanked them very prettily. But when their leader, Brontes, tried to take her on his knee, she tore a great handful of hair from his chest. He put her down quickly and went away cursing.

Holding her silver bow high, screaming with joy, she raced across field and valley and hill, followed by her nymphs who streamed after her with flashing knees and floating hair laughing and singing. She came to Arcadia where Pan was feeding his hounds.

"Oh, Pan," she cried. "Oh, little king of the wood, my favorite cousin, please give me some of your dogs — the best ones, please."

"And what will you give me in return?" he said, looking at the nymphs.

"Choose," she said. "But I should warn you, cousin, that like me they have taken an unbreakable vow of chastity."

"Never mind," said Pan. "Keep them. What dogs do you fancy?"

"That one and that one and that one," she cried. "And this one. And I must have him . . . and him."

He gave her his ten best dogs. Three of them were huge black and white hounds able to catch a live lion and drag it back to the hunter. The others were lean white deerhounds; any one of them could outrun a stag.

Artemis was wild to try out her new gifts. She sent her white hounds racing after two deer, bidding them bring back the animals unharmed. She harnessed the deer to her silver chariot and drove away. She saw a tree which had been struck by lightning; it was still smoldering. She had her nymphs break pine branches and thrust them into the cinders, for night was coming and she wanted light to shoot by. She was too impatient to wait for dawn.

Four times she shot her silver bow. First she split a pine tree, then an olive tree. Then she shot a wild boar. Lastly, she shot an arrow into a city of unjust men, and the arrow pierced all of them, never ceasing its flight till they were all dead.

And the people, seeing her ride over the mountains, wielding her silver bow, followed by the maidens and their torches, called her the Goddess of the Moon. Some called her the Maiden of the Silver Bow. Others called her Lady of the Wild Things. Some called her the Huntress. Others, simply, the Maiden. And so she had her last gift — many names.

She let no man approach her. Once a young man named Actaeon glimpsed her bathing in a stream. She was so beautiful he could not bear to go away, but hid there, watching. She saw him, and immediately changed him into a stag. Then she whistled up her hounds, who tore him to pieces.

She tried to impose the same rule upon her nymphs, which was difficult. Zeus himself seduced one of the most beautiful, named Callisto. When Artemis learned of this, she changed Callisto into a she-bear and whistled to her dogs. They came leaping and howling and would have torn the bear to pieces too, but Zeus happened to notice what was going on. He caught Callisto up and set her among the stars, still in her bear shape so that Hera would not be suspicious.

Once Artemis found her vow difficult to keep. But that is another story, the story of Oranos, which comes later.

Apollo was the most beautiful of the gods. His hair was dark gold, his eyes stormy blue. He wore a tunic of golden panther skin, carried his golden bow, and wore a quiver of golden arrows. His chariot was beaten gold; its horses were white with golden manes and flame-colored eyes. He was god of the sun always. Later he became patron of music, poetry, mathematics, and medicine. And, later, when he was a mature god, he preached moderation. He bade his worshippers to look first into their own hearts and find there the beginnings of wisdom, and to conduct themselves prudently in all things. But in his youth he did many cruel and wanton deeds. Several times he was almost expelled from the company of the gods by Zeus whom he had angered with his wild folly.

As soon as he was given his bow and arrows he raced down from Olympus to hunt the Python who had hunted his mother. Dryads, who are tattletales, told him he could find his enemy at Mount Parnassus. There he sped. As he stood on a hill, he saw the great serpent weaving its dusty coils far below. He notched an arrow, drew his bow, and let fly. It darted like light; he saw it strike, saw the huge coils flail in agony. Shouting with savage glee he raced down the slope, but when he got there he found the serpent gone. It had left a trail of blood which he followed to the oracle of Mother Earth at Delphi. Python was hiding in a cave, where he could not be followed. Apollo breathed on his arrow heads and shot them into the cave as fast as he could. They broke into flames when they hit. Smoke filled the cave, and the serpent had to crawl out. Apollo, standing on a rock, shot him so full of arrows he looked like a porcupine. He skinned the great snake and saved the hide for a gift.

Now it was a sacred place where he had done his killing; here lived the oracles of Mother Earth, whom the gods themselves consulted. They were priestesses, trained from infancy. They chewed laurel, built fires of magic herbs, and sat in the smoke, which threw them into a trance wherein they saw — and told in riddles — what was to come. Knowing that he had already violated a shrine, Apollo thought he might as well make his deed as large as possible, and claimed the oracles for his own — bidding them prophesy in his name.

When Mother Earth complained to Zeus about the killing of her Python, Apollo smoothly promised to make amends. He instituted annual games at Delphi in celebration of his victory, and these he graciously named after his enemy, calling them the Pythian games. And he named the oracles Pythonesses.

Less excusable was Apollo's treatment of a satyr named Marsyas. This happy fellow had the misfortune to be an excellent musician — a realm Apollo considered his own — and where he would brook no rivalry. Hearing the satyr praised too often, Apollo invited him to a contest. The winner was to choose a penalty to which the loser would have to submit, and the Muses were to judge. So Marsyas played his flute and Apollo played his lyre. They played exquisitely; the Muses could not choose between them. Then Apollo shouted, "Now you must turn your instrument upside down, and play and sing at the same time. That is the rule. I go first." Thereupon the god turned his lyre upside down, and played and sang a hymn praising the gods, and especially their beautiful daughters, the Muses. But you cannot play a flute upside down, and certainly cannot sing while playing it, so Marsyas was declared the loser. Apollo collected his prize. He flayed Marsyas alive, and nailed his skin to a tree. A stream gushed from the tree's roots and became a river. On the banks of that river grew reeds which sang softly when the wind blew. People called the river Marsyas, and that is still its name.

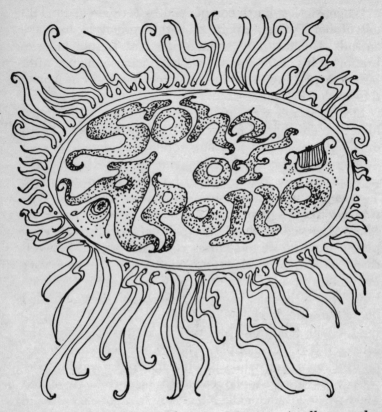

During the contest with the satyr Marsyas, Apollo won the
favor of the most playful Muse, Thalia, queen of festivities.
With her he fathered the Corybantes, or crested dancers,
lithe young men who shaved their hair to a forelock and
danced at the great rituals.

Then, roaming the hillsides, he came across a young
girl who reminded him of his sister. She was a huntress.
She chased deer on foot, hunted bears and wolves. When
he saw her wrestling a full-grown lion, and throwing it

to earth, he decided he must have her. Her name was Cyrene. The son he gave her was named Aristeus, who taught man beekeeping, olive culture, cheese-making, and many other useful arts.

His next adventure was with the nymph Dryope. He found her tending sheep on a mountainside. He hid behind a tree and watched her. To his dismay, she was joined by a gaggle of hamadryads, mischievous girls who love to tell tales. So he had to stay hidden. He waited for the hamadryads to leave, but they lingered. Gods are impatient; they hate to be kept waiting. He changed himself into a tortoise and crawled out. The nymphs were delighted to see him, and turned him this way and that, and tickled him with a straw. He was a splendid glossy tortoise with a beautiful black and green shell. Dryope wanted him for her own, and put him in her tunic. When her friends protested, he turned himself into a snake, poked his head out of the tunic, and hissed at them. The hamadryads fled, screaming. Dryope fainted. When she came to, she was in the arms of a god. The son he gave her was Amphissus, founder of cities, and builder of temples.

But his most famous son was Asclepius. This was the manner of his birth.

Apollo fell in love with Coronis, a princess of Thessaly, and insisted on having his way, which was unwise of him because she loved an Arcadian prince named Ischys. When she was with child, Apollo went on a journey, but set a white crow to spy on her. All crows were white then, and were excellent chaperons; they had sharp eyes and jeering voices.

It was to Delphi that Apollo had gone. An oracle there told him that at that very moment Coronis was entertaining young Ischys. Just then the crow flew in, wildly excited, full of scandal, telling the same tale. "Your fault! You did not watch her closely enough!" cried Apollo. And he cursed the crow with a curse so furious that her feathers were scorched — and all crows have been black ever since.

Apollo could not bring himself to kill Coronis. So he asked his sister Artemis to oblige him. She was happy to; she was never fond of his amours. She sped to Thessaly, and finished Coronis with one arrow.

Apollo, very dejected, put the corpse on the funeral pyre and lighted the fire. Then he remembered that she was with child by him. Hermes, who was standing by waiting to conduct her soul to Tartarus (that was one of his duties), understood the situation in a flash. He delivered the dead girl of a living child, a boy. Apollo wished to have nothing to do with the child, and asked Hermes to take care of him. Hermes had been struck by the way the baby had observed the details of his own birth — watching everything with a wide stare, so interested he forgot to cry — and recognized that this was an unusual child. So he gave him into the care of Chiron, the centaur, the fabulous tutor. Chiron taught him diagnostics, surgery, herbology, and hunting.

The boy could not wait to grow up. He doctored everyone he could get his hands on, and was soon known throughout the land for his skill at curing the sick. His fame reached Apollo, who decided to test him. He appeared at Asclepius's door in the guise of a feeble old man afflicted with every loathsome disease known to medicine — and a pauper besides. Asclepius tended him with his own hands, and was so gentle and skillful that Apollo was amazed. The god resumed his own form and embraced the lad and told him he was pleased with his progress. He sent him to see his aunt Athene, who, he said, knew certain secrets of mortality. She too approved of the young man, and gave him two vials of Gorgon blood. One vial could raise the dead, the other was the deadliest poison ever known. "No, Aunt," he said. "I need only the first vial. You keep the other."

Some say that it was by his own skill that he restored life to the dead, and that Athene was simply trying to take some of the credit for herself. Be that as it may, he did snatch several patients from the very gates of Tartarus, and Hades was enraged. He complained to his brother Zeus that Asclepius was robbing him. Zeus stood on Olympus, hurled a thunderbolt, and killed the young physician together with the patient he was tending.

When Apollo heard about this, he went into one of his wild heedless rages, stormed to Olympus, battered in the doors of Hephaestus' smithy, and there slew all the Cyclopes, who had forged the thunderbolt which had killed his son. When Zeus heard this, he banished Apollo to Tartarus forever. But Mother Leto came and pleaded with him, reminding him of their old love. She spoke so beautifully that Zeus relented, withdrew the edict of Apollo's banishment, and even agreed to bring Asclepius back to life. But he suggested that Asclepius be more tactful about his cures, and avoid offending the gods.

When Aphrodite heard this story, she was bitten by envy. She considered herself a favorite of Zeus, but he had never done so much for her. Her heart was bitter against Apollo, and she wanted to do him a mischief. She called her son Eros, the infant archer, whose sweetly poisoned arrows infect man and woman with a most dangerous fever. She told him what she wanted.

Eros had two kinds of arrows — one tipped with gold and tailed with white dove feathers; these were for love. The others, made of lead, with brown owl feathers, were the arrows of indifference. He took up his bow and stalked his game.

Apollo, he knew, was hunting, so he made his path cross that of Daphne, a mountain nymph, daughter of the river god Penaeus. Then, fluttering above them, invisible, he shot Apollo with the dart of love and Daphne with the arrow of indifference. When the golden god came running down the slope toward the nymph, he saw her start up and run away. He could not understand it. She fled; the god pursued. She was a very swift runner, but great footsteps pounded behind her, and she felt the heat of his breath on her shoulders.

She ran toward the river, and cried, "Oh, Father, save me! Save me!" And her father heard. Apollo, reaching for her, found himself hugging a tree; the rough bark scratched his face. He said, "But why? . . . Why do you hate me so?"

The wind blew through the leaves, and they whispered, "I don't know. . . . I don't know. . . ."

But then the tree took pity on the grieving god and gave him a gift — a wreath of her leaves, laurel leaves, that would never wither — to crown heroes, and poets, and young men who win games.

And still, today, when questioned by losers, laurel trees whisper, "I don't know. . . . I don't know. . . ."

Young gods were often precocious, but no one so much as Hermes who, five minutes after his birth, sneaked out of his crib and went searching for adventure. He toddled swiftly down the slope of Mount Cyllene until he came to a meadow where he saw a herd of beautiful white cows grazing. He saw no cowherd, and decided to steal them. A treeful of crows began to seethe and whistle, "They belong to Apollo . . . to Apollo . . . 'pollo . . . ," but he paid them no heed. He plaited grass into shoes for the cows, and fitted them over their hooves, and drove them away.

When Apollo returned, he was furious to see his cows gone, and even more furious when he searched for tracks and found none — only odd sweeping marks on the ground. The crows chattered, "A baby stole them . . . your brother, your brother . . ." But this made no sense to Apollo; besides he did not trust crows. He did not know where to begin looking; he searched far and wide, but could find no clue.

Then one morning he passed a cave he had passed a hundred times before. But this time he heard strange, beautiful sounds coming out of it — sounds unlike anything he had ever heard before — and he looked inside. There, drowsing by the fire, was a tall lovely Titaness named Maia, whom he had seen before in the garden on Olympus. Sitting in her lap was a little baby boy, doing something to a large tortoise shell from which the strange sounds seemed to be coming.

"Good day, cousin," said Apollo. "Are you to be congratulated on a new son?"

"Hail, bright Phoebus," said Maia. "May I have the honor of presenting your half-brother, young Hermes?"

"Half-brother, eh? Well, that's an honor without being a distinction. What's that he's playing with?"

"He makes his own toys," said Maia proudly. "He's so clever, you can't imagine. He made this out of an old shell that he strung with cowgut, and from it he draws the most ravishing sounds. Listen . . ."

"Cowgut? May I ask what cow he persuaded to contribute her vital cords for his pastime?"

"I do not understand your question, cousin."

"Understand this, cousin. I have had a herd of cows stolen recently. The crows told me they had been taken by some baby, my brother, but I didn't believe them. I seem to owe them an apology."

"What?" cried Maia. "Are you accusing this innocent babe of being a cattle thief? For shame!"

"Mother, if you don't mind," said a clear little voice, "perhaps you'd better let me handle this." The baby stood on his mother's knee, and bowed to Apollo. "I did take your cows, brother. But I didn't know they were yours. How could I have? And they are quite safe, except for one. Wishing to begin my life with an act of piety, I sacrificed her to the twelve gods."

"Twelve gods?" said Apollo haughtily. "I am acquainted with but eleven."

"Yes, sir," said Hermes. "But I have the honor to be the twelfth. Above all things, I wish your good will, fair brother. So, in return for this cow, allow me to make you a present — this instrument. I call it a lyre. I'll be glad to teach you to play."

Apollo was enchanted with the trade. He stayed in the cave all that afternoon practicing his scales. As he was strumming his new toy, he noticed Hermes cutting reeds, which the child swiftly tied together, notched in a certain way, then put to his lips, and began to make other sounds, even more beautiful than the lyre could produce.

"What's that?" cried Apollo. "What do you call that? I want that too."

"I don't need any more cows," said Hermes.

"I must have it. What else of mine do you wish?"

"Your golden staff."

"But this is my herdsman's staff. Do you not know that I am the god of herdsmen, and that this is the rod of authority?"

"A minor office," said Hermes. "Unworthy of the lord of the sun. Perhaps you would allow me to take over the chore. Give me your golden staff, and I will give you these pipes."

"Agreed! Agreed!"

"But since pipes and lyre together will make you god of music, I must have something to boot. Teach me augury."

"You drive a hard bargain for a nursling," said Apollo. "I think you belong on Olympus, brother. This cave will not long offer scope for your talents."

"Oh, yes, take me there!" cried Hermes. "I am eager to meet Father Zeus."

So Apollo took Hermes to Olympus, and introduced him to his father. Zeus was intrigued by the wit and impudence of the child. He hid him away from Hera, and spent hours conversing with him.

"You say you wish to enter the Pantheon," said Zeus. "But really — all the realms and powers seem to have been parceled out."

"Father, I am of modest nature," said Hermes. "I require no vast dignities. Only a chance to be useful, to serve you, and to dwell in your benign and potent presence. Let me be your herald. Let me carry your tidings. You will find me quick and resourceful, and what I can't remember I will make up. And, I guarantee, your subjects will get the message."

"Very well," said Zeus. "I will give you a trial."

So Hermes became the messenger god, and accomplished his duties with such swiftness, ingenuity, and cheerfulness that he became a favorite of his father, who soon rewarded him with other posts. Hermes became patron of liars and thieves and gamblers, god of commerce, framer of treaties, and guardian of travelers. Hades became his client too, and called upon him to usher the newly dead from earth to Tartarus.

He kept a workshop on Olympus, and there invented the alphabet, astronomy, and the scales; also playing cards and card games. He carried Apollo's golden staff decorated with white ribbons, wore a pot-shaped hat, and winged sandals which carried him through the air more swiftly than any bird could fly.

It was he who gave Zeus the idea of disguising himself and mingling with mortals when bored with Olympus. He joined his father in this, and they had many adventures together . . . which will be told in their place.

No one celebrated the birth of Hephaestus. His mother, Hera, had awaited him with great eagerness, hoping for a child so beautiful, so gifted, that it would make Zeus forget his heroic swarm of children from lesser consorts. But when the baby was born she was appalled to see that he was shriveled and ugly, with an irritating bleating wail. She did not wait for Zeus to see him, but snatched the infant up and hurled him off Olympus.

For a night and a day he fell, and hit the ground at

the edge of the sea with such force that both of his legs were broken. He lay there on the beach mewing piteously, unable to crawl, wracked with pain, but unable to die because he was immortal. Finally, the tide came up. A huge wave curled him under its arm and carried him off to sea. And there he sank like a stone, and was caught by the playful Thetis, a naiad, who thought he was a tadpole.

When Thetis understood it was a baby she had caught, she made a pet of him, and kept him in her grotto. She was amazed at the way the crippled child worked shells and bright pebbles into jewelry. One day she appeared at a great festival of the gods wearing a necklace he had made. Hera noticed the ornament, and praised it, and asked her how she had come by it. Thetis told her of the strange twisted child whom someone had dropped into the ocean, and who lived now in her cave making wonderful jewels. Hera divined that it was her own son, and demanded him back.

Hephaestus returned to Olympus. There Hera presented him with a broken mountain nearby, where he could set up forges and bellows. She gave him the brawny Cyclopes to be his helpers, and promised him Aphrodite as a bride, if he would labor in the mountain and make her fine things. Hephaestus agreed because he loved her, and excused her cruelty to him.

"I know that I am ugly, Mother," he said, "but the fates would have it so. And I will make you gems so beautiful for your tapering arms and white throat and black hair that you will forget my ugliness sometimes, and rejoice that you have taken me back from the sea."

He became the smith-god, the great artificer, lord of mechanics. And the mountain always smoked and rumbled with his toil.

Aphrodite was the goddess of love and beauty; so there are more stories told about her than anyone else, god or mortal. Being what she is, she enters other stories; and such is the power of her magic girdle that he who even speaks her name falls under her spell, and seems to glimpse her white shoulders and catch the perfume of her golden hair. And he loses his wits and begins to babble, and tells the same story in many ways.

But all the tales agree that she is the goddess of desire, and, unlike other Olympians, is never distracted from

　　THE GREEK GODS: THE PANTHEON

her duties. Her work is her pleasure, her profession, her hobby. She thinks of nothing but love, and nobody expects more of her.

She was born out of the primal murder. When Cronos butchered his father, Oranos, with the scythe his mother had given him, he flung the dismembered body off Olympus into the sea, where it floated, spouting blood and foam which drifted, whitening in the sun. From the foam rose a tall beautiful maiden, naked and dripping. Waves attended her. Poseidon's white horses brought her to the island of Cythera. Wherever she stepped, the sand turned to grass and flowers bloomed. Then she went to Cyprus. Hillsides burst into flowers, and the air was full of birds.

Zeus brought her to Olympus. She was still dripping from the sea. She wore nothing but the bright tunic of her hair which fell below her knees and was yellow as daffodils. She looked about the great throne room where the gods were assembled to meet her, arched her throat and laughed with joy.

Hera was watching Zeus narrowly. "You must marry her off," she whispered. "At once — without delay!"

"Yes," said Zeus. "Some sort of marriage would seem to be indicated."

And he said, "Brothers, sons, cousins, Aphrodite is to be married. She will choose her own husband. So make your suit."

The gods closed around her, shouting promises, pressing their claims. Earth-shaking Poseidon swung his mighty trident to clear a space about himself. "I claim you for the sea," he said. "You are sea-born, foam-born, and belong to me. I offer you grottos, riddles, gems, fair surfaces, dark surroundings. I offer you variety. Drowned sailors, typhoons, sunsets. I offer you secrets. I offer you riches that the earth does not know — power more subtle, more fluid than the dull fixed land. Come with me — be queen of the sea."

He slammed his trident on the floor, and a huge green tidal wave swelled out of the sea — high, high as Olympus, curling its mighty green tongue as if to lick up the mountain — and poised there, quivering, not breaking, as the gods gaped. Then Poseidon raised his trident, and the mighty wave subsided like a ripple. He bowed to Aphrodite. She smiled at him, but said nothing.

Then the gods spoke in turn, offering her great gifts. Apollo offered her a throne and a crown made of hottest sun-gold, a golden chariot drawn by white swans, and the Muses for her handmaids. Hermes offered to make her queen of the crossways where all must come — where she would hear every story, see every traveler, know each deed — a rich pageant of adventure and gossip so that she would never grow bored.

She smiled at Apollo and Hermes and made no answer.

Then Hera, scowling, reached her long white arm and dragged Hephaestus, the lame smith-god, from where he had been hiding behind the others, ashamed to be seen. And she hissed into his ear, "Speak, fool. Say exactly what I told you to say."

He limped forward with great embarrassment, and stood before the radiant goddess, eyes cast down, not daring to look at her. He said: "I would make a good husband for a girl like you. I work late."

Aphrodite smiled. She said nothing, but put her finger under the chin of the grimy little smith, raised his face, leaned down, and kissed him on the lips.

That night they were married. And at the wedding party she finally spoke — whispering to each of her suitors — telling each one when he might come with his gift.

nature myths

Prometheus was a young Titan, no great admirer of Zeus. Although he knew the great lord of the sky hated explicit questions, he did not hesitate to beard him when there was something he wanted to know.

One morning he came to Zeus, and said, "O Thunderer, I do not understand your design. You have caused the race of man to appear on earth, but you keep him in ignorance and darkness."

"Perhaps you had better leave the race of man to me,"

**PROMETHEUS**

said Zeus. "What you call ignorance is innocence. What you call darkness is the shadow of my decree. Man is happy now. And he is so framed that he will remain happy unless someone persuades him that he is unhappy. Let us not speak of this again."

But Prometheus said, "Look at him. Look below. He crouches in caves. He is at the mercy of beast and weather. He eats his meat raw. If you mean something by this, enlighten me with your wisdom. Tell me why you refuse to give man the gift of fire."

Zeus answered, "Do you not know, Prometheus, that every gift brings a penalty? This is the way the Fates weave destiny — by which gods also must abide. Man does not have fire, true, nor the crafts which fire teaches. On the other hand, he does not know disease, warfare, old age, or that inward pest called worry. He is happy, I say, happy without fire. And so he shall remain."

"Happy as beasts are happy," said Prometheus. "Of what use to make a separate race called man and endow him with little fur, some wit, and a curious charm of unpredictability? If he must live like this, why separate him from the beasts at all?"

"He has another quality," said Zeus, "the capacity for worship. An aptitude for admiring our power, being puzzled by our riddles, and amazed by our caprice. That is why he was made."

"Would not fire and the graces he can put on with fire make him more interesting?"

"More interesting, perhaps, but infinitely more dangerous. For there is this in man too: a vaunting pride that needs little sustenance to make it swell to giant size. Improve his lot, and he will forget that which makes him pleasing — his sense of worship, his humility. He will grow big and poisoned with pride and fancy himself a god, and before we know it, we shall see him storming Olympus. Enough, Prometheus! I have been patient with you, but do not try me too far. Go now, and trouble me no more with your speculations."

Prometheus was not satisfied. All that night he lay awake making plans. Then he left his couch at dawn, and standing tiptoe on Olympus, stretched his arm to the eastern horizon where the first faint flames of the sun were flickering. In his hand he held a reed filled with a dry fiber; he thrust it into the sunrise until a spark smoldered. Then he put the reed in his tunic and came down from the mountain.

At first men were frightened by the gift. It was so hot, so quick; it bit sharply when you touched it, and for pure spite made the shadows dance. They thanked Prometheus, and asked him to take it away. But he took the haunch of a newly killed deer and held it over the fire. And when the meat began to sear and sputter, filling the cave with its rich smells, the people felt themselves melting with hunger, and flung themselves on the meat and devoured it greedily, burning their tongues.

"This that I have brought you is called 'fire,'" Prometheus said. "It is an ill-natured spirit, a little brother of the sun, but if you handle it carefully it can change your whole life. It is very greedy; you must feed it twigs, but only until it becomes a proper size. Then you must stop, or it will eat everything in sight, and you too. If it escapes, use this magic: water. It fears the water spirit, and if you touch it with water, it will fly away until you need it again."

He left the fire burning in the first cave, with children staring at it wide-eyed, and then went to every cave in the land.

Then, one day, Zeus looked down from the mountain

and was amazed. Everything had changed. Man had come out of his cave. Zeus saw woodmen's huts, farmhouses, villages, walled towns, even a castle or two. He saw men cooking their food, carrying torches to light their way at night. He saw forges blazing, men beating out ploughs, keels, swords, spears. They were making ships and raising white wings of sails and daring to use the fury of the winds for their journeys. They were wearing helmets, riding out in chariots to do battle, like the gods themselves.

Zeus was full of rage. He seized his largest thunderbolt. "So they want fire," he said to himself. "I'll give them fire — more than they can use. I'll turn their miserable little ball of earth into a cinder." But then another thought came to him, and he lowered his arm. "No," he said to himself, "I shall have vengeance — and entertainment too. Let them destroy themselves with their new skills. This will make a long twisted game, interesting to watch. I'll attend to them later. My first business is with Prometheus."

He called his giant guards, and had them seize Prometheus, drag him off to the Caucasus, and there bind him to a mountain peak with great chains specially forged by Hephaestus — chains which even a Titan in agony could not break. And when the friend of man was bound to the mountain, Zeus sent an eagle to hover about him forever, tearing at his belly, and eating his liver.

Men knew a terrible thing was happening on the mountain, but they did not know what. But the wind shrieked like a giant in torment, and, sometimes, like fierce birds.

Many centuries he lay there — until another hero was born brave enough to defy the gods. He climbed to the peak in the Caucasus, and struck the shackles from Prometheus, and killed the eagle. His name was Heracles.

After Zeus had condemned Prometheus to his long torment for having given man fire, he began to plan how to punish man for having accepted it.

Finally, he hit upon a scheme. He ordered Hephaestus to mold a girl out of clay, and to have Aphrodite pose for it to make sure it was beautiful. He breathed life into the clay figure, the clay turned to flesh, and she lay sleeping, all new. Then he summoned the gods, and asked them each to give her a gift.

Apollo taught her to sing and play the lyre. Athene taught her to spin, Demeter to tend a garden. Aphrodite taught her how to look at a man without moving her eyes, and how to dance without moving her legs. Poseidon gave her a pearl necklace and promised she would never drown. And, finally, Hermes gave her a beautiful golden box, which, he told her, she must never, never open. And then Hera gave her curiosity.

Hermes took her by the hand and led her down the slope of Olympus. He led her to Epimetheus, brother of Prometheus, and said, "Father Zeus grieves at the disgrace which has fallen upon your family. And to show you that he holds you blameless in your brother's offense, he makes you this gift — this girl, fairest in all the world. She is to be your wife. Her name is Pandora, the all-gifted."

So Epimetheus and Pandora were married. Pandora spun and baked and tended her garden, and played the lyre and danced for her husband, and thought herself the happiest young bride in all the world. Only one thing bothered her — the golden box. First she kept it on the table and polished it every day so that all might admire it. But the sunlight lanced through the window, and the box sparkled and seemed to be winking at her.

She found herself thinking, "Hermes must have been teasing. He's always making jokes; everyone knows that. Yes, he was teasing, telling me never to open his gift. For if it is so beautiful outside, what must it be inside? Why, he has hidden a surprise for me there. Gems more lovely than have ever been seen, no doubt. If the box is so rich, the gift inside must be even more fine — for that is the way of gifts. Perhaps Hermes is *waiting* for me to open the box and see what is inside, and be delighted, and thank him. Perhaps he thinks me ungrateful. . . ."

THE GREEK GODS: NATURE MYTHS

But even as she was telling herself this, she knew it was not so — that the box must not be opened — that she must keep her promise.

Finally, she took the box from the table, and hid it in a dusty little storeroom. But it seemed to be burning there in the shadows. Its heat seemed to scorch her thoughts wherever she went. She kept passing that room, and stepping into it, making excuses to dawdle there. Sometimes she took the box from its hiding place and stroked it, then quickly shoved it out of sight, and rushed out of the room.

She took it then, locked it in a heavy oaken chest, put great shackles on the chest, and dug a hole in her garden. She put the chest in, covered it over, and rolled a boulder on top of it. When Epimetheus came home that night, her hair was wild and her hands were bloody, her tunic torn and stained. But all she would tell him was that she had been working in the garden.

That night the moonlight blazed into the room. She could not sleep. The light pressed her eyes open. She sat up in bed and looked around. All the room was swimming in moonlight. Everything was different. There were deep shadows and swaths of silver, all mixed, all moving. She arose quietly and tiptoed from the room.

She went out into the garden. The flowers were blowing, the trees were swaying. The whole world was adance in the magic white fire of that moonlight. She walked to the rock and pushed it. It rolled away as lightly as a pebble. And she felt herself full of wild strength.

She took a shovel and dug down to the chest. She unshackled it, and drew out the golden box. It was cold, cold; coldness burned her hand to the bone. She trembled. What was inside that box seemed to know the very secret of life, which she must look upon or die.

She took the little golden key from her tunic, fitted it into the keyhole, and gently opened the lid. There was a swarming, a hot throbbing, a wild meaty rustling, and a foul smell. Out of the box, as she held it up in the moonlight, swarmed small scaly lizardlike creatures with bat wings and burning red eyes.

They flew out of the box, circled her head once, clapping their wings and screaming thin little jeering screams — and then flew off into the night, hissing and cackling.

Then, half-fainting, sinking to her knees Pandora, with her last bit of strength, clutched the box and slammed down the lid — catching the last little monster just as it was wriggling free. It shrieked and spat and clawed her hand, but she thrust it back into the box and locked it in. Then she dropped the box, and fainted away.

What were those deathly creatures that flew out of the golden box? They were the ills that beset mankind: the spites, disease in its thousand shapes, old age, famine, insanity, and all their foul kin. After they flew out of the box they scattered — flew into every home, and swung from the rafters — waiting. And when their time comes they fly and sting — and bring pain and sorrow and death.

At that, things could have been much worse. For the creature that Pandora shut into the box was the most dangerous of all. It was foreboding, the final spite. If it had flown free, everyone in the world would have been told exactly what misfortune was to happen every day of his life. No hope would have been possible. And so there would have been an end to man. For, though he can bear endless trouble, he cannot live with no hope at all.

Long ago, when the world was very new, two boys were racing along the edge of a cliff that hung over a deep blue sea. They were the same size; one boy had black hair, the other had yellow hair. The race was very close. Then the yellow-haired one spurted ahead, and won the race. The loser was very angry.

"You think you're pretty good," he said. "But you're not so much. My father is Zeus."

"My father is Apollo," said the yellow-haired boy, whose name was Phaethon.

"My father is the chief god, king of the mountain, lord of the sky."

"My father is lord of the sun."

"My father is called the thunderer. When he is angry, the sky grows black and the sun hides. His spear is a lightning bolt, and that's what he kills people with. He hurls it a thousand miles and it never misses."

"Without my father there would be no day. It would always be night. Each morning he hitches up his horses and drives the golden chariot of the sun across the sky. And that is daytime. Then he dives into the ocean stream, and boards a golden ferryboat and sails back to his eastern palace. That time is called night."

"Sometimes I visit my father," said Epaphus, the other boy. "I sit on Olympus with him, and he teaches me things, and gives me presents. Know what he gave me last time? A little thunderbolt just like his — and he taught me how to throw it. I killed three vultures, scared a fishing boat, started a forest fire. Next time I go, I'll throw it at more things. Do you visit your father?"

Phaethon never had. But he could not bear to tell Epaphus. "Certainly," he said, "very often. I go to the eastern palace, and he teaches me things too."

"What kind of things? Has he taught you to drive the horses of the sun?"

"Oh, yes. He taught me to handle their reins, and how to make them go, and how to make them stop. And they're huge horses. Tall as this mountain. They breathe fire."

"I think you're making it all up," said Epaphus. "I can tell. I don't even believe there is a sun chariot. There's the sun, look at it. It's not a chariot."

"Oh, what you see is just one of the wheels," said Phaethon. "There's another wheel on the other side. The body of the chariot is slung between them. That is where the driver stands and whips his horses. You cannot see it because your eyes are too small, and the glare is too bright."

"Well," said Epaphus. "Maybe it is a chariot, but I still don't believe your father lets you drive it. In fact, I don't believe you've been to the palace of the sun. I doubt that Apollo would know you if he saw you. Maybe he isn't even your father. People like to say they're descended from the gods, of course. But how many of us are there, really?"

"I'll prove it to you," cried Phaethon, stamping his foot. "I'll go to the palace of the sun right now and hold my father to his promise. I'll show you."

"What promise?"

"He said I was getting to be so good a charioteer that next time he would let me drive the sun chariot *alone*. All by myself. From dawn to night. Right across the sky. And this time is next time."

"Poof — words are cheap," said Epaphus. "How will I know it's you driving the sun? I won't be able to see you from down here."

"You'll know me," said Phaethon. "When I pass the village I will come down close and drive in circles around your roof. You'll see me all right. Farewell."

"Are you starting now?"

"Now. At once. Just watch the sky tomorrow, son of Zeus."

And he went off. He was so stung by the words of his friend, and the boasting and lying he had been forced to do, that he traveled night and day, not stopping for food or rest, guiding himself by the morning star and the evening star, heading always east. Nor did he know the way. For, indeed, he had never once seen his father Apollo. He knew him only through his mother's stories. But he did know that the palace must lie in the east, because that is where he saw the sun start each morning. He walked on and on, until, finally, he lost his way completely, and weakened by hunger and exhaustion, fell swooning in a great meadow by the edge of a wood.

Now, while Phaethon was making his journey, Apollo sat in his great throne room on a huge throne made of gold and rubies. This was the quiet hour before dawn when night left its last coolness upon the earth. And it was then, at this hour, that Apollo sat on his throne, wearing a purple cloak embroidered with the golden signs of the zodiac. On his head, a crown given him by the dawn goddess, made of silver and pearls. A bird flew in the window and perched on his shoulder and spoke to him. This bird had sky-blue feathers, golden beak, golden claws, and golden eyes. It was one of Apollo's sun hawks. It was this bird's job to fly here and there gathering gossip. Sometimes she was called the spy bird.

Now she said, "Apollo, I have seen your son!"

"Which son?"

"Phaethon. He's coming to see you. But he has lost his way and lies exhausted at the edge of the wood. The wolves will surely eat him. Do you care?"

"I will have to see him before I know whether I care. You had better get back to him before the wolves do. Bring him here in comfort. Round up some of your companions, and bring him here as befits the son of a god."

The sun hawk seized the softly glowing rug at the foot of the throne and flew away with it. She summoned three of her companions, and they each took a corner of the rug. They flew over a desert and a mountain and a wood and came to the field where Phaethon lay. They flew down among the howling of wolves, among burning eyes set in a circle about the unconscious boy. They pushed him onto the rug, and each took a corner in her beak, and flew away.

Phaethon felt himself being lifted into the air. The cold wind of his going revived him, and he sat up. People below saw a boy sitting with folded arms on a carpet rushing through the cold, bright moonlight far above their heads. It was too dark, though, to see the birds, and that is why we hear tales of flying carpets even to this day.

Phaethon was not particularly surprised to find himself in the air. The last thing he remembered was lying down on the grass. Now, he knew, he was dreaming. A good dream — floating and flying — his favorite kind. And when he saw the great cloud castle on top of the mountain, all made of snow and rose in the early light, he was more sure than ever that he was dreaming. He saw sentries in flashing golden armor, carrying golden spears. In the courtyard he saw enormous woolly dogs with fleece like clouddrift guarding the gate. These were Apollo's great sun hounds, ancestors of our own Skye terriers.

Over the wall flew the carpet, over the courtyard, through the tall portals. And it wasn't until the sun hawks gently let down the carpet in front of the throne that he began to think that this dream might be very real. He raised his eyes shyly and saw a tall figure sitting on the throne. Taller than any man, and appallingly beautiful to the boy — with his golden hair and stormy blue eyes and strong laughing face. Phaethon fell on his knees.

"Father," he cried. "I am Phaethon, your son!"

"Rise, Phaethon. Let me look at you."

He stood up, his legs trembling.

"Yes, you may well be my son. I seem to see a resemblance. Which one did you say?"

"Phaethon."

"Oh, Clymene's boy. I remember your mother well. How is she?"

"In health, sire."

"And did I not leave some daughters with her as well? Yellow-haired girls — quite pretty?"

"My sisters, sire. The Heliads."

"Yes, of course. Must get over that way and visit them all one of these seasons. And you, lad — what brings you to me? Do you not know that it is courteous to await an invitation before visiting a god — even if he is in the family?"

"I know, Father. But I had no choice. I was taunted by a son of Zeus, Epaphus. And I would have flung him over the cliff and myself after him if I had not resolved to make my lies come true."

"Well, you're my son, all right. Proud, rash, accepting no affront, refusing no adventure. I know the breed. Speak up, then. What is it you wish? I will do anything in my power to help you."

"Anything, Father?"

"Anything I can. I swear by the river Styx, an oath sacred to the gods."

"I wish to drive the sun across the sky. All by myself. From dawn till night."

Apollo's roar of anger shattered every crystal goblet in the great castle.

"Impossible!" he cried. "No one drives those horses but me. They are tall as mountains. Their breath is fire. They are stronger than the tides, stronger than the wind. It is all that *I* can do to hold them in check. How can your puny grip restrain them? They will race away with the chariot, scorching the poor earth to a cinder."

"You promised, Father."

"Yes, I promised, foolish lad. And that promise is a death warrant. A poor charred cinder floating in space — well, that is what the oracle predicted for the earth, but I did not know it would be so soon . . . so soon."

"It is almost dawn, Father. Should we not saddle the horses?"

"Will you not withdraw your request — allow me to preserve my honor without destroying the earth? Ask me anything else, and I will grant it. Do not ask me this."

"I have asked, sire, and you have promised. And the hour for dawn comes, and the horses are unharnessed. The sun will rise late today, confusing the wise."

"They will be more than confused when this day is done," said Apollo. "Come."

Apollo took Phaethon to the stable of the sun, and there the boy saw the giant fire-white horses being harnessed to the golden chariot. Huge they were. Fire-white with golden manes and golden hooves and hot yellow eyes. When they neighed, the trumpet call of it rolled across the sky — and their breath was flame. They were being harnessed by a Titan, a cousin of the gods, tall as a tree, dressed in asbestos armor with helmet of tinted crystal against the glare. The sun chariot was an open shell of gold. Each wheel was the flat round disk of the sun as it is seen in the sky. And Phaethon looked very tiny as he stood in the chariot. The reins were thick as bridge cables, much too large for him to hold, so Apollo tied them around his waist. Then Apollo stood at the head of the team gentling the horses, speaking softly to them, calling them by name — Pyroeis, Eous, Aethon, Phlegon.

"Good lads, good horses, go easy today, my swift ones. Go at a slow trot and do not leave the path. You have a new driver today."

The great horses dropped their heads to his shoulder and whinnied softly, for they loved him. Phaethon saw the flame of their breath play about his head, saw Apollo's face shining out of the flame. But he was not harmed, for he was a god, and could not be hurt by physical things.

He came to Phaethon, and said, "Listen to me, son. You are about to start a terrible journey. Now, by the obedience you owe me as a son, by the faith you owe a god, by my oath that cannot be broken, and your pride that will not bend, I put this rule upon you: Keep the middle way. Too high and the earth will freeze, too low and it will burn. Keep the middle way. Give the horses their heads; they know the path, the blue middle course of day. Drive them not too high, nor too low, but above all, do not stop. Or you will fire the air about you where you stand, charring the earth and blistering the sky. Do you heed me?"

"I do, I do!" cried Phaethon. "Stand away, sire! The dawn grows old and day must begin! Go, horses, go!"

And Apollo stood watching as the horses of the sun went into a swinging trot, pulling behind them the golden chariot, climbing the first eastern steep of the sky.

At first things went well. The great steeds trotted easily along their path across the high blue meadow of the sky. And Phaethon thought to himself, "I can't understand why my father was making such a fuss. This is easy. For me, anyway. Perhaps I'm a natural-born coachman though. . ."

He looked over the edge of the chariot. He saw tiny houses down below, and specks of trees. And the dark blue puddle of the sea. The coach was trundling across the sky. The great sun wheels were turning, casting light, warming and brightening the earth, chasing all the shadows of night.

"Just imagine," Phaethon thought, "how many people now are looking up at the sky, praising the sun, hoping the weather stays fair. How many people are watching me, me, me . . . ?" Then he thought, "But I'm too small to see. They can't even see the coach or the horses — only the great wheel. We are too far and the light is too bright. For all they know, it is Apollo making his usual run. How can they know it's me, me, me? How will my mother know, and my sisters? They would be so proud. And Epaphus — above all, Epaphus — how will *he* know? I'll come home tomorrow after this glorious journey, and tell him what I did, and he will laugh at me, and tell me I'm lying, as he did before. And how shall I prove it to him? No, this must not be. I must show him that it is I driving the chariot of the sun — I alone. Apollo said not to come too close to earth, but how will he know? And I won't stay too long — just dip down toward our own village and circle his roof three times — which is the signal we agreed upon. After he recognizes me, I'll whip up the horses, and resume the path of the day."

He jerked on the reins, pulled the horses' heads down. They whinnied angrily, and tossed their heads. He jerked the reins again.

"Down" he cried. "Down! Down!"

The horses plunged through the bright air, golden hooves twinkling, golden manes flying, dragging the great glittering chariot after them in a long flaming swoop. When they reached his village, he was horrified to see the roofs bursting into fire. The trees burned. People rushed about screaming. Their loose clothing caught fire, and they burned like torches as they ran.

Was it his village? He could not tell because of the smoke. Had he destroyed his own home? Burned his mother and his sisters?

He threw himself backward in the chariot, pulling at the reins with all his might, shouting, "Up! Up!"

And the horses, made furious by the smoke, reared on their hind legs in the air. Then leaped upward, galloping through the smoke, pulling the chariot up, up.

Swiftly the earth fell away beneath them. The village was just a smudge of smoke. Again he saw the pencil-stroke of mountains, the inkblot of seas. "Whoa!" he cried. "Turn now! Forward on your path!" But he could no longer handle them. They were galloping, not trotting. They had taken the bit in their teeth. They did not turn toward the path of the day across the meadow of the sky, but galloped up, up. And the people on earth saw the sun shooting away until it was no larger than a star.

Darkness came. And cold. The earth froze hard. Rivers froze, and oceans. Boats were caught fast in the ice in every sea. It snowed in the jungle. Marble buildings cracked. It was impossible for anyone to speak; breath froze on the speakers' lips. And in village and city, in the field and in the wood, people died of the cold. And the bodies piled up where they fell, like firewood.

Still Phaethon could not hold his horses, and still they galloped upward dragging light and warmth away from the earth. Finally, they went so high that the air was too thin to breathe. Phaethon saw the flame of their breath which had been red and yellow burn blue in the thin air. He himself was gasping for breath; he felt the marrow of his bones freezing.

Now the horses, wild with change, maddened by the feeble hand on the reins, swung around and dived toward earth again. Now all the ice melted, making great floods. Villages were swept away by a solid wall of water. Trees were uprooted and whole forests were torn away. The fields were covered by water. Lower swooped the horses, and lower yet. Now the water began to steam — great billowing clouds of steam as the water boiled. Dead fish floated on the surface. Naiads moaned in dry riverbeds.

Phaethon could not see; the steam was too thick. He had unbound the reins from his waist, or they would have cut him in two. He had no control over the horses at all. They galloped upward again — out of the steam — taking at last the middle road, but racing wildly, using all their tremendous speed. Circling the earth in a matter of minutes, smashing across the sky from horizon to horizon, making the day flash on and off like a child playing with a lamp. And the people who were left alive were bewildered by the light and darkness following each other so swiftly.

Up high on Olympus, the gods in their cool garden heard a clamor of grief from below. Zeus looked upon earth. He saw the runaway horses of the sun and the hurtling chariot. He saw the dead and the dying, the burning forests, the floods, the weird frost. Then he looked again at the chariot and saw that it was not Apollo driving, but someone he did not know. He stood up, drew back his arm, and hurled a thunderbolt.

It stabbed through the air, striking Phaethon, killing him instantly, knocking him out of the chariot. His body, flaming, fell like a star. And the horses of the sun, knowing themselves driverless, galloped homeward toward their stables at the eastern edge of the sky.

Phaethon's yellow-haired sisters grieved for the beautiful boy. They could not stop weeping. They stood on the bank of the river where he had fallen, until Apollo, unable to comfort them, changed them into poplar trees. Here they still stand on the shore of the river, weeping tears of amber sap.

And, since that day, no one has been allowed to drive the chariot of the sun except the sun god himself. But there are still traces of Phaethon's ride. The ends of the earth are still covered with icecaps. Mountains still rumble, trying to spit out the fire started in their bellies by the diving sun.

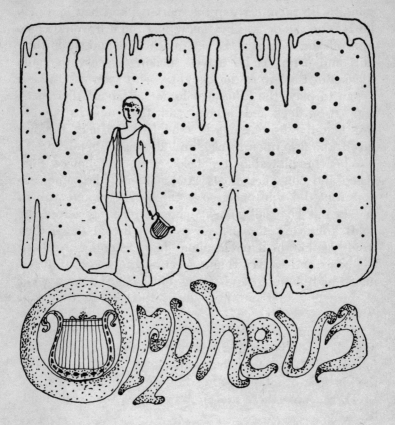

His father was a Thracian king; his mother, the Muse
Calliope. For awhile he lived on Parnassus with his mother
and his eight beautiful aunts, and there met Apollo who
was courting the laughing Muse Thalia. Apollo was taken
with Orpheus and gave him a little golden lyre, and
taught him to play. And his mother taught him to make
verses for singing.

So he grew up to be a poet and musician such as the
world had never known. Fishermen used to coax him to go

sailing with them early in the morning, and had him play his lyre on the deck. They knew that the fish would come up from the depths of the sea to hear him and sit on their tails and listen as he played, making it easy to catch them. But they were not caught, for as soon as Orpheus began to play, the fishermen forgot all about their nets, and sat on deck and listened with their mouths open — just like the fish. And when he had finished, the fish dived, the fishermen awoke, and all was as before.

When he played in the fields, animals followed him, sheep and cows and goats. And not only the tame animals, but the wild ones too — the shy deer, and wolves, and bears. They all followed him, streaming across the fields, following him, listening. When he sat down they would gather in a circle about him, listening. Nor did the bears and wolves think of eating the sheep until the music had stopped, and it was too late. And they went off growling to themselves about the chance they had missed.

And as he grew and practiced, he played more and more beautifully, so that now not only animals but trees followed him as he walked, wrenching themselves out of the earth and hobbling after him on their twisted roots. In Thrace now there are circles of trees that still stand, listening.

People followed him too, of course, as he strolled about, playing and singing. Men and women, boys and girls — particularly girls. But as time passed and the faces changed, he noticed that one face was always there. She was always there — in front, listening — when he played. She became especially noticeable because she began to appear among his other listeners — among the animals and the trees who listened as he played. So that, finally, he knew, that wherever he might be, wherever he might strike up his lyre and raise his voice in song, whether people were listening, or animals, or trees and rocks — she would be there — very slender and still with huge dark eyes and long black hair, her face like a rose.

Then one day he took her aside and spoke to her. Her name was Eurydice. She said she wanted to do nothing but be where he was, always; and that she knew she could not hope for him to love her, but that would not stop her from following him, and serving him in any way she could. She would be happy to be his slave if he wanted her to.

Now this is the kind of thing any man likes to hear in any age, particularly a poet. And, although Orpheus was admired by many women and could have had his choice, he decided that he must have this one, so much like a child still, with her broken murmurs and great slavish eyes. And so he married her.

They lived happily, very happily, for a year and a day. They lived in a little house near the river in a grove of trees that pressed close, and they were so happy that they rarely left home. People began to wonder why Orpheus was never seen about, why his wonderful lyre was never heard. They began to gossip, as people do. Some said Orpheus was dead, killed by the jealous Apollo for playing so well. Others said he had fallen in love with a river nymph, had gone into the water after her, and now lived at the bottom of the river, coming up only at dawn to blow tunes upon the reeds that grew thickly near the shore. And others said that he had married dangerously, that he lived with a sorceress, who with her enchantments made herself so beautiful that he was chained to her side, and would not leave her even for a moment.

Finally, it was the last rumor that people chose to believe. Among them was a visitor — Aristeus, a young king of Athens, Apollo's son by the nymph Cyrene — and a mighty hunter. Aristeus decided that he must see this beautiful enchantress, and stationed himself in the grove of trees, and watched the house. For two nights and two days he watched. Then, finally, he saw a girl come out. She made her way through the grove and went down the path toward the river. He followed. When he reached the river, he saw her there, taking off her tunic.

Without a word, he charged toward her, crashing like a wild boar through the trees. Eurydice looked up, and saw a stranger hurtling toward her. She fled. Swiftly she ran — over the grass toward the trees. She heard him panting after her. She doubled back toward the river, and ran, heedless of where she was going. Wild to escape, she stepped full on a nest of coiled and sleeping snakes, who awoke immediately and bit her leg in so many places that she was dead before she fell. And Aristeus, rushing up, found her lying in the reeds.

He left her body where he found it. There it lay until Orpheus, looking for her, came at dusk, and saw her glimmering whitely like a fallen birch. By this time, Hermes had come and gone, taking her soul with him to Tartarus. Orpheus stood looking down at her. He did not weep. He touched a string of his lyre once, absently, and it sobbed. But only once — he did not touch it again. He kept looking at her. She was pale and thin, her hair was disheveled, her legs streaked with mud. She seemed more childish than ever. He looked down at her, dissatisfied with the way she looked, as he felt when he set a wrong word in a verse. She was wrong this way. She did not belong dead. He would have to correct it. He turned abruptly, and set off across the field.

He entered Tartarus at the nearest place, a passage in

the mountains called Aornos, and walked through a cold mist until he came to the river Styx. He saw shades waiting there to be ferried across, but not Eurydice. She must have crossed before. The ferry came back and put out its plank, and the shades went on board, each one reaching under his tongue for the penny to pay the fare. But the ferryman, Charon, huge and swart and scowling, stopped Orpheus when he tried to embark.

"Stand off!" he cried. "Only the dead go here."

Orpheus touched his lyre and began to sing — a river song, a boat song, about streams running in the sunlight, and boys making twig boats, and then growing up to be young men who go in boats, and how they row down the river thrusting with powerful young arms, and what the water smells like in the morning when you are young, and the sound of oars dipping.

And Charon, listening, felt himself carried back to his own youth — to the time before he had been taken by Hades and put to work on the black river. And he was so lost in memory that the great sweep oar fell from his hand, and he stood there, dazed, tears streaming down his face — and Orpheus took up the oar, and rowed across.

The shades filed off the ferry and through the gates of Tartarus. Orpheus followed them. Then he heard a hideous growling. An enormous dog with three heads, each one uglier than the next, slavered and snarled. It was the three-headed dog Cerberus, who guarded the gates of Tartarus.

Orpheus unslung his lyre and played. He played a dog song, a hound song, a hunting song. In it was the faint far yapping of happy young hounds finding a fresh trail —dogs with one graceful head in the middle where it should be, dogs that run through the light and shade of the forest chasing stags and wolves, as dogs should do, and are not forced to stand forever before dark gates, barking at ghosts.

Cerberus lay down, and closed his six eyes, lolled his three tongues, and went to sleep to dream of the days when he had been a real dog, before he had been captured and changed and trained as a sentinel for the dead. Orpheus stepped over him, and went through the gates.

Through the Field of Asphodel he walked, playing. The shades twittered thin glee like bats giggling. Sisyphus stopped pushing his stone, and the stone itself poised on the side of the hill to listen, and did not fall back. Tantalus heard, and stopped lunging his head at the water; the music laved his thirst. Minos, and Rhadamanthys, and Aeacus, the great judges of the dead, heard the music on their high benches, and fell dreaming about the old days on Crete where they had been young princes, about the land battles and the sea battles and the white bulls and the beautiful maidens and the flashing swords, and all the days gone by. They sat there, listening, eyes blinded with tears, deaf to litigants.

Then Hades, king of the underworld, lord of the dead, knowing his great proceedings disrupted, waited sternly on his throne as Orpheus approached.

"No more cheap minstrel tricks," he cried. "I am a god. My rages are not to be assuaged, nor my decrees nullified. No one comes to Tartarus without being sent for. No one has before, and no one will again, when the tale is told of the torments I intend to put you to."

Orpheus touched his lyre and sang a song that conjured up a green field, and a grove of trees, and a slender girl painting flowers, and all the light about her head, with the special clearness there was when the world had

THE GREEK GODS: NATURE MYTHS

just begun. He sang of how that girl made a sight so pleasing as she played with the flowers that the birds overhead gossiped of it, and the moles underground — until the word reached even gloomy Tartarus, where a dark king heard, and went up to see for himself. Orpheus sang of that king seeing the girl for the first time in a great wash of early sunlight, and what he felt when he saw that stalk-slender child in her tunic and green shoes moving with her paintpot among the flowers, of the fever that ran in his blood when first he put his mighty arm about her waist, and drank her screams with his dark lips, and tasted her tears; of the grief that had come upon him when he almost lost her again to her mother by Zeus's decree; and of the joy that filled him when he learned that she had eaten of the pomegranate.

Persephone was sitting at Hades' side. She began to cry. Hades looked at her. She leaned forward and whispered to him swiftly. The king turned to Orpheus. Hades did not weep, but no one had ever seen his eyes so brilliant.

"Your verse has affected my queen," he said. "Speak. We are disposed to hear. What is it you wish?"

"My wife."

"What have we to do with your wife?"

"She is here. She was brought here today. Her name is Eurydice. I wish to take her back with me."

"Never done," said Hades. "A disastrous precedent."

"Not so, great Hades," said Orpheus. "This one stroke of unique mercy will illumine like a lightning flash the caverns of your dread decree. Nature exists by proportion, and perceptions work by contrast, and the gods themselves are part of nature. This brilliant act of kindness, I say, will make cruelty seem like justice for all the rest of time. Pray give me back my wife again, great monarch. For I will not leave without her — not for all the torments that can be devised."

He touched his lyre once again, and the Eumenides, hearing the music, flew in on their hooked wings, their brass claws tinkling like bells, and poised in the air above Hades' throne. The terrible hags cooed like doves, saying, "Just this once, Hades. Let him have her. Let her go."

Hades stood up then, black-caped and towering. He looked down at Orpheus, and said, "I must leave the laurel leaves and the loud celebrations to my bright nephew Apollo. But I, even I, of such dour repute, can be touched by eloquence. Especially when it attracts such unlikely advocates. Hear me then, Orpheus. You may have your wife. She will be given into your care, and you will conduct her yourself from Tartarus to the upper light. But if, during your journey, you look back once, only once — if, for any reason whatever you turn your eyes from where you are headed and look back toward where you were — then my leniency is revoked, and Eurydice will be taken from you again, and forever. Go. . . ."

Orpheus bowed, once to Hades, once to Persephone, lifted his head and smiled a half-smile at the hovering Furies, turned and walked away. Hades gestured. And as Orpheus walked through the fields of Tartarus, Eurydice fell into step behind him. He did not see her. He thought she was there, he was sure she was there. He thought he could hear her footfall, but the black grass was thick; he could not be sure. But he thought he recognized her breathing — that faint sipping of breath he had heard so many nights near his ear; he thought he heard her breathing, but the air again was full of the howls of the tormented, and he could not be sure.

But Hades had given his word; he had to believe — and so he visualized the girl behind him, following him as he led. And he walked steadily, through the Field of Asphodel toward the gates of Tartarus. The gates opened as he approached. Cerberus was still asleep in the middle of the road. He stepped over him. Surely he could hear her now, walking behind him. But he could not turn around to see, and he could not be sure because of the cry of vultures which hung in the air above the river Styx like gulls over a bay. Then, on the gangplank, he heard a footfall behind him, surely. . . . Why, oh why, did she walk so lightly? Something he had always loved, but he wished her heavier-footed now.

He went to the bow of the boat and gazed sternly ahead, clenching his teeth, and tensing his neck until it became a thick halter of muscle so that he could not turn his head. On the other side, climbing toward the passage of Aornos, the air was full of the roaring of the great cataracts that fell chasm-deep toward Styx, and he could not hear her walking, and he could not hear her breathing. But he kept a picture of her in his mind, walking behind him, her face growing more and more vivid with excitement as she approached the upper air. Then, finally, he saw a blade of light cutting the gloom, and knew that it was the sun falling through the narrow crevasse which is Aornos, and that he had brought Eurydice back to earth.

But had he? How did he know she was there? How did he know that this was not all a trick of Hades? Who calls the gods to judgment? Who can accuse them if they lie? Would Hades, implacable Hades, who had had the great Asclepius murdered for pulling a patient back from death, would that powerful thwarting mind that had imagined the terrain of Tartarus, and the bolts of those gates, and dreamed a three-headed dog — could such a mind be turned to mercy by a few notes of music, a few tears? Would he who made the water shrink always from the thirst of Tantalus, and who toyed with Sisyphus' stone, rolling it always back and forth — could this will, this black ever-curdling rage, this dire fancy, relent and let a girl return to her husband just because the husband had asked? Had it been she following him through the Field of Asphodel, through the paths of Tartarus, through the gates, over the river? Had it been she or the echoes of his own fancy — that cheating mourner's fancy, which, kind but to be cruel, conjures up the beloved face and voice only to scatter them like smoke? Was it this, then? Was this the final cruelty? Was this the torment Hades had promised? Was this the final ironic flourish of death's scepter, which had always liked to cudgel poets? Had he come back without her? Was it all for nothing? Or was she there? Was she there?

Swiftly he turned, and looked back. She was there. It was she. He reached his hand to take hers and draw her out into the light — but the hand turned to smoke. The arm turned to smoke. The body became mist, a spout of mist. And the face melted. The last to go was the mouth with its smile of welcome. Then it melted. The bright vapor blew away in the fresh upper current of air that blew through the crevasse from the upper world.

# Narcissus & Echo

Of all the nymphs of river and wood, a dryad named Echo
was the best beloved. She was not only very beautiful
and very kind, but had a haunting musical voice. The
other dryads and naiads and creatures of the wood begged
her to sing to them and tell them stories — and she did.
She was a great favorite of Aphrodite who used to come
all the way from Olympus to chat with Echo and listen
to her tales. Being goddess of love, she was especially con-
cerned with gossip — which is mostly about who loves

whom and what they are doing about it. And Echo kept her entertained as no one else could.

Aphrodite said, "All the world asks me for favors, Echo. But not you. Tell me, is there not someone you would wish to love you? Some man, boy, god? Just name him, and I will send my son Eros, who will shoot him with his arrow, and make him fall madly in love with you."

But Echo laughed, and said, "Alas, sweet Aphrodite, I have seen no man who pleases me. And gods are too fickle. Man and boy — I look at them all very carefully, but none seems beautiful enough to match my secret dream. When the time comes, I shall ask your help — if it ever comes."

"Well, you are lovely enough to demand the best," said Aphrodite. "On the other hand, the best happens only once. And who can wait so long? However, I am always at your service."

Now Echo did not know this, but at that moment the most beautiful boy in the whole world was lost in that very wood, trying to find his way out. His name was Narcissus, and he was so handsome that he had never been able to speak to any woman except his mother. For any girl who saw him immediately fainted. Of course this also gave him a very high opinion of himself. And, as he went through the woods, he thought:

"Oh, how I wish I could find someone as beautiful as I. I will not be friends with anyone less perfect in face or form. Why should I? This leaves me lonely, true, but it's better than lowering myself."

So he walked along the path, but he was going the wrong way, getting more and more lost. In the other part of the wood Echo had just said farewell to Aphrodite, and was coming back to the hollow tree in which she lived. She came to a glade in the forest, and there saw something that made her stop in astonishment, and hide behind a tree. For whom did she see but Zeus himself — king of the gods, lord of the sky. He was leaning on his volt-blue lightning shaft, holding a river nymph by the shoulder, and she was smiling up at him.

"Well," said Echo. "He's at it again. Won't Aphrodite enjoy hearing about *this!*"

But then her attention was caught by something else. She turned to see a tall purple-clad figure moving through the trees toward the glade. She recognized Hera, queen of the gods, jealous wife of Zeus, and she realized that Hera must have heard of what Zeus was doing, and was coming to catch him. And so the kind-hearted nymph hurried forward and curtsied low before Hera, saying, "Greetings, great queen. Welcome to the wood."

"Hush, fool!" whispered Hera. "Don't say a word! I am trying to take someone by surprise."

"This is a proud day for us," said Echo, thinking swiftly, "to be visited by so many gods. Just two minutes ago, Zeus was here looking for you."

"Zeus? Looking for *me?* Are you sure?"

"The great Zeus. Your husband. He asked me whether I had seen you. Said he had heard you were coming this way, and he wished very much to meet you. When I told him I had not seen you, he flew off looking very disappointed."

"Really? Can it be so? Zeus looking for me? Disappointed? Well — miracles never cease. Which way did he go?"

"Oh . . . toward Olympus."

"Thank you, child," said Hera. "I'll be going too."

And she disappeared.

In the meantime, Zeus, hearing voices, had hidden

himself and the river nymph in the underbrush. When Hera left, he came out, and to thank Echo he gave her a shining blue sapphire ring from his own finger.

Hera, having returned to Olympus, found that Zeus was not there. She realized that something was wrong, and sped back to the forest. The first thing she saw was Echo admiring a large sapphire ring that burned on her finger like a fallen star. Hera recognized the ring, and immediately understood that the nymph had tricked her in some way and had been given the ring as a reward.

"Wretched creature!" she cried. "I know what you have done. I see the gift you have been given. And I would not have it said that my husband is more generous than I. So I too shall reward you for what you have done. Because you have used your voice for lying, you shall never be able to say anything to anyone again — except the last words that have been said to you. Now, try lying."

"Try lying," said Echo.

"No more shall you meddle in high concerns — no more shall you gossip and tell stories and sing songs — but endure this punishment evermore. . . ."

"Evermore . . ." said Echo, sobbing.

And Hera went away to search for Zeus. And the nymph, weeping, rushed toward her home in the hollow tree. As she was going she saw once again the dazzling brightness that was the face of a god, and she stopped to see. It was no god, but a lad about her own age, with black hair and eyes the color of the sapphire Zeus had given her. When she saw him, all the grief of her punishment dissolved, and she was full of a great laughing joy. For here was the boy she had been looking for all her life, as beautiful as her secret dream . . . a boy she could love.

She danced toward him. He stopped, and said, "Pardon me, but can you show me the path out of the wood?"

"Out of the wood . . ." said Echo.

"Yes," he said. "I'm lost. I've been wandering here for hours, and I can't seem to find my way out of the wood."

"Out of the wood . . ."

"Yes. I've told you twice. I'm lost. Can you help me find the way?"

"The way . . ."

"Are you deaf, perhaps? Why must I repeat everything?"

"Repeat everything . . ."

"No, I will not! It's a bore! I won't do it!"

"Do it . . ."

"Look I can't stand here arguing with you. If you don't want to show me the way, well then, I'll just try to find someone who can."

"Who can . . ."

Narcissus glared at her, and started away. But she came to him, and put her arms around him, and tried to kiss his face.

"Oh, no — none of that!" said Narcissus, shoving her away. "You're just like all the rest of them, aren't you? They faint, and you say stupid things. Stop it! You can't kiss me."

"Kiss me . . ."

"No!"

"No . . ."

And she tried to kiss him again. Again he pushed her aside. She fell on her knees on the path, and hugged his legs, and lifted her lovely tear-streaked face to his, trying to speak. But she could not.

"No!" he said. "Let go! You can't hold me here. I will not love you."

"Love you . . ."

He tore himself from her grip and strode away. "Farewell," he called.

"Farewell . . ."

She looked after him until he disappeared. And when he was gone she felt such sadness, such terrible tearing grief, such pain in every part of her, that it seemed she was being torn apart by white-hot little pincers, torn flesh from bone. And since she could not speak, she said this prayer to herself:

"Oh, Aphrodite . . . fair goddess . . . you promised me a favor. Do me one now. Hear me though I am voiceless. My love has disappeared, and I must disappear too, for I cannot bear the pain."

And Aphrodite, in the garden on Olympus, heard this prayer — for prayers do not have to be spoken to be heard. She looked down upon the grieving nymph, and pitied her, and made her disappear. Her body melted into thin cool air, so that the pain was gone. All was gone . . . except her voice, for Aphrodite could not bear to lose the sound of that lovely story-telling voice. The goddess said, "I grant you your wish — and one thing more. You have not asked vengeance upon the love that has betrayed you. You are too sweet and kind. But *I* shall take vengeance, nevertheless. I decree now that whoever has caused you this pain will know the same terrible longing. He will fall in love with someone who cannot return his love . . . and will forever desire and never achieve."

But Narcissus knew nothing of this — of Echo's grief, nor Aphrodite's vow. He wandered the forest path, thinking, "All these girls who love me on sight — it's too bad I cannot find one as beautiful as I. For until I do, I shall not love. And all their loving will be only vexation to me."

He sat down on the bank of a river to rest. Not a river really, but a finger of the river — a clear little stream moving slowly through rocks. The sun shone on it; it became a mirror, holding the trees and the sky upside down, and a small silver trembling sun. And Narcissus, looking into the stream, saw a face.

He blinked his eyes, and looked again. It was still there — the most beautiful face he had ever seen. As beautiful, he knew, as his own, but with a nimbus of light behind it so that the hair was blurred and looked long — like a girl's. He gazed and gazed, and could not have enough of it. He knew that he could look upon this face forever and still not be satisfied. He put out his hand to touch her. The water trembled, and she disappeared.

"A water nymph," he thought. "A lovely dryad . . . daughter of the river god, no doubt. The loveliest of his daughters. She is shy. Like me, she can't bear to be touched. Ah . . . here she is again."

The face looked at him out of the stream. Again, very timidly, he reached his hand. Again the water trembled and the face disappeared.

"I will stay here until she loves me," he said to himself. "She may hide now, but presently she will recognize me too. And come out." And he said aloud: "Come out, lovely one."

And the voice of Echo, who had followed him to the stream, said, "Lovely one . . ."

"Hear that, hear that!" cried Narcissus, overjoyed. "She cares for me too. You do, don't you? You love me."

"Love me . . ."

"I do . . . I do . . . Finally I have found someone to love. Come out, come out. . . . Oh, will you never come out?"

"Never come out . . ." said Echo.

"Don't say that, please don't say that. Because I will stay here till you do. This, I vow."

"I vow . . ."

"Your voice is as beautiful as your face. And I will stay here, adoring you forever."

"Forever . . ."

And Narcissus stayed there, leaning over the stream, watching the face in the water, watching, watching . . . sometimes pleading with it to come out, hearing its voice answer. Coaxing, begging, looking. . . . Day after day he stayed there, night after night, never moving, never eating, never looking away from the face. He stayed there so long that his legs grew into the bank of the river, and became roots. His hair grew long, tangled, leafy. And his pale face and blue eyes became delicate blue and white petals — the flower Narcissus, that lives on the river-bank, and leans over watching its reflection in the water.

And there you can find it till this day. And in the woods too, when all is still, you will sometimes come upon Echo. And if you call to her in a certain way, she will answer your call.

There was a king who had three daughters, and the youngest, named Psyche, was so beautiful that Aphrodite grew jealous, and began to plan mischief.

"I'll teach that little upstart," she said to herself. "How dare she go around pretending to be as beautiful as I? When I get through with her she'll wish she'd been born ugly as a toad."

She called her son Eros to her, and said, "Son, your mother has been insulted. See that castle down there?

In a bower there, a maiden lies asleep. You must go pierce her with one of your arrows."

"While she is asleep? What good will it do?"

"No good at all. Just evil, which is exactly what I plan for her."

"But she can fall in love only with the one she is looking at when the arrow pierces her. Why bother when she is asleep?"

"Because if you scratch her with the arrow while she sleeps, she will form a passion for the first one she sees when she awakes. And I will take care to supply her with someone very special — the castle dwarf, perhaps. Or the gardener, who has just celebrated his hundred-and-second birthday. Or a donkey — yes, that's possible too. I haven't decided. But you can be sure it will be someone quite undesirable. Her family will be surprised."

"This is a cruel trick, Mother."

"Oh, yes — it's meant to be cruel. I tell you the girl has irritated me. Now be off and do your work."

Obediently, Eros flew down to the castle. He made himself invisible, and flew through the window into the girl's chamber. He stood looking at her.

"She is very beautiful," he thought. "Too beautiful for her own safety, poor girl."

He leaned over her, holding his dart so as to delicately scratch her shoulder. But he must have made some sound, for she opened her eyes then and looked straight into his, although she could not see him. And her huge black brilliant eyes startled him so that the dart slipped and he scratched his own hand. He stood there feeling the sweet poison spread in his veins, confused, growing dizzy with joy and strangeness. He had spread love, but never felt it, shot others, but never been wounded himself. And he did not know himself this way.

The girl closed her eyes and went to sleep again. He stood looking at her. Suddenly she had become the most wonderful, the most curious, the most valuable thing in the world to him. And he knew that he would never let her come to any harm if he could prevent it. He thrust his dart into his quiver and flew back to Olympus.

When he told his mother what had happened she fell into a rage and ordered him out of her sight. She then flung a curse upon Psyche. She cast an invisible hedge of thorns about her, so that no suitor could come near. The beautiful young princess became very lonely, and very sad. Her father and mother could not understand why no one offered to marry her.

Now the gods often quarrel, but Olympus had never seen such a feud as now flared between Aphrodite and her son.

"How dare you torment the girl like that?" he said to his mother. "So long as you keep this spell upon her, I will do no business of love. I will shoot no one with my arrows. Your praises will not be sung. And without praise you will dry up and become a vicious old harpy. Farewell."

And indeed Eros refused to shoot his arrows. People stopped falling in love with one another. There was no praise for Aphrodite; her temples stood empty, her altars unadorned. No marriages were made, no babies born. The world seemed to grow old and dull in a day. Without love, work dried. Farmers did not plough their fields. Ships crawled listlessly on the seas. Fishermen scarcely cast their nets. Indeed, there were not many fish to catch, for they had sunk sullenly to the very bottom of the sea. And Aphrodite herself, goddess of love and beauty, found herself wasting in the great parching despair that came off the earth like a desert wind.

EROS AND PSYCHE

She called her son to her, and said, "I see that you must have your way. What is it you wish?"

"The girl," he said.

"You shall have her. Sharpen your darts now, and get back to work or we shall all run melancholy mad."

So Eros filled his quiver with arrows, stood upon a low cloud, and shot as fast as he could. And man and woman awakened to each other again. Fish leaped in the sea. Stallions trumpeted in the field. Sounds of the earth holding revel came to the goddess on the mountain, and she smiled.

But the parents of Psyche still grieved. For now with all the world celebrating the return of love, and the most unlikely people getting married, still no one asked for their daughter. They went to the oracle, who said:

"Psyche is not meant for mortal man. She is to be the bride of him who lives on the mountain and vanquishes both man and god. Take her to the mountain, and say farewell."

As the king and queen understood this, they thought that their daughter was intended for some monster, who would devour her as so many other princesses had been devoured to appease the mysterious forces of evil. They dressed her in bridal garments and hung her with jewels and led her to the mountain. The whole court followed, mourning, as though it were a funeral instead of a wedding.

Psyche herself did not weep. She had a strange dreaming look on her face. She seemed scarcely to know what was going on. She said no word of fear, wept no tear, but kissed her mother and father good-bye, and waited on the mountain, standing tall, her white bridal gown blowing about her, her arms full of flowers. The wedding party returned to the castle. The last sound of their voices faded. She stood there listening to a great silence. The wind blew hard, hard. Her hair came loose. The gown whipped about her like a flag. She felt a great pressure upon her, and she did not understand. Then a huge breathy murmur, the wind itself howling in her ear, seemed to say, "Fear not. I am Zephyrus, the west wind, the groom's messenger. I have come to take you home."

She listened to the soft howling, and believed the words she seemed to hear, and was not afraid, even though she felt herself being lifted off the mountain, felt herself sailing through the air like a leaf. She saw her own castle pass beneath her, and thought, "If they're looking up and see me now, they'll think that I'm a gull." And she was glad that they would not know her.

Past low hills, over a large bay, beyond forests and fields and another ring of hills, the wind took her. And now she felt herself coasting down steeps of air, through the failing light, through purple clumps of dusk, toward another castle, gleaming like silver on a hilltop. Gently, gently, she was set down within the courtyard. It was empty. There were no sentries, no dogs, nothing but shadows, and the moon-pale stones of the castle. She saw no one. But the great doors opened. A carpet unreeled itself and rolled out to her feet. She walked over the carpet, through the doors. They closed behind her.

A torch burned in the air, and floated in front of her. She followed it. It led her through a great hallway into a room. The torch whirled. Three more torches whirled in to join it, then stuck themselves in the wall and burned there, lighting the room. It was a smaller room, beautifully furnished. She stepped onto the terrace which looked out over the valley toward the moonlit sea.

A table floated into the room, and set itself down solidly on its three legs. A chair placed itself at the table. Invisible hands began to set the table with dishes of gold and goblets of crystal shells. Food appeared on the plates, and the goblets filled with purple wine.

"Why can I not see you?" she cried to the invisible servants.

A courteous voice said, "It is so ordered."

"And my husband? Where is he?"

"Journeying far. Coming near. I must say no more."

She was very hungry after her windy ride. She ate the food and drank the wine. The torch then led her out of the room to another room that was an indoor pool, full of fragrant warm water. She bathed herself. Fleecy towels were offered her, a jeweled comb, and a flask of perfumed oil. She anointed herself, went back to her room, and awaited her husband.

Presently, she heard a voice in the room. A powerful voice speaking very softly, so softly that the words were like her own thoughts.

"You are Psyche. I am your husband. You are the most beautiful girl in all the world, beautiful enough to make the goddess of love herself grow jealous."

She could not see anyone. She felt the tone of the voice press hummingly upon her as if she were in the center of a huge bell.

"Where are you?"

"Here."

She reached out her arms. She felt mighty shoulders, hard as marble, but warm with life. She felt herself being enfolded by great muscular arms. And a voice spoke: "Welcome home."

A swoon of happiness darkened her mind. The torches went out, one by one.

When she awoke next morning, she was alone. But she was so happy she didn't care. She went dancing from room to room, exploring the castle, singing as she went. She sang so happily that the great pile of stone was filled with the sound of joy. She explored the castle, the court-yard, and the woods nearby. One living creature she found, a silvery greyhound, dainty as a squirrel and fierce as a panther. She knew it was hers. He went exploring the woods with her, and showed her how he could out-race the deer. She laughed with joy to see him run.

At the end of the day she returned to the castle. Her meal was served by the same invisible servants. She again bathed and anointed herself. At midnight again her husband spoke to her, and she embraced him, and won-dered how it was that of all the girls in the world she had been chosen for this terrible joy.

Day after day went by like this, and night after night. And each night he asked her, "Are you happy, little one? Can I bring you anything, give you anything?"

"Nothing, husband, nothing. Only yourself."

"That you have."

"But I want to see you. I want to see the beauty I hold in my arms."

"That will be, but not yet. It is not yet time."

"Whatever you say, dear heart. But then, can you not stay with me by day as well, invisible or not. Why must you visit me only at night?"

"That too will change, perhaps. But not yet. It is too soon."

"But the day grows so long without you. I wait for nightfall so, it seems it will never come."

"You are lonely. You want company. Would you like your sisters to visit you?"

"My sisters . . . I have almost forgotten them. How strange."

"Do you care to renew your acquaintance?"

"Well, perhaps. But I don't really care. It is you I want. I want to see you. I want you here by day as well as by night."

"You may expect your sisters here tomorrow."

The next day the west wind bore Psyche's elder sisters to the castle, and landed them in the courtyard, wind blown and bewildered. They were fearful at having been snatched away from their own gardens, and relieved to find themselves deposited so gently in the courtyard. How much more amazed they were, then, to see their own sister, whom they thought long dead, running out of the castle. She was more beautiful than ever, blooming with happiness, more richly garbed than any queen. She stormed joyously out of the castle, swept them into her arms, embraced and kissed them, and made them greatly welcome.

Then she led them into the castle. The invisible servants bathed and anointed them, and served them a sumptuous meal. And with every new wonder they saw, with every treasure their sister showed them, they grew more and more jealous. They too had married kings, but little local ones, and this castle made theirs look like dog kennels. They did not eat off golden plates and drink out of jewels. Their servants were the plain old visible kind. And they ate and drank with huge appetites, and grew more and more displeased with every bite.

"But where is your husband?" said the eldest one. "Why

is he not here to welcome us? Perhaps he didn't want us to come."

"Oh, he did, he did," cried Psyche. "It was his idea. He sent his servant, the west wind, for you."

"Oho," sniffed the second sister. "It is he we have to thank for being taken by force and hurled through the air. Pretty rough transport."

"But so swift," said Psyche. "Do you not like riding the wind? I love it."

"Yes, you seem to have changed considerably," said the eldest. "But that's still not telling us where your husband is. It is odd that he should not wish to meet us . . . very odd."

"Not odd at all," said Psyche. "He — he is rarely here by day. He — has things to do."

"What sort of things?"

"Oh, you know. . . . Wars, peace treaties, hunting . . . you know the things that men do."

"He is often away then?"

"Oh, no! No . . . that is . . . only by day. At night he returns."

"Ah, then we will meet him tonight. At dinner, perhaps . . ."

"No . . . well . . . he will not be here. I mean — he will, but you will not see him."

"Just what I thought!" cried the eldest. "Too proud to meet us. My dear, I think we had better go home."

"Yes, indeed," said the second sister. "If your husband is too high and mighty to give us a glimpse of his august self, then we're plainly not wanted here."

"Oh, no," said Psyche. "Please listen. You don't understand."

"We certainly do not."

And poor Psyche, unable to bear her sisters' barbed hints, told them how things were. The two sisters sat at the table, listening. They were so fascinated they even forgot to eat, which was unusual for them.

"Oh, my heavens!" cried the eldest, "It's worse than I thought."

"Much much worse," said the second. "The oracle was right. You *have* married a monster."

"Oh, no, no!" cried Psyche. "Not a monster! But the most beautiful creature in the world!"

"Beautiful creatures like to be seen," said the eldest. "It is the nature of beauty to be seen. Only ugliness hides itself away. You have married a monster."

"A monster," said the second. "Yes, a monster . . . a dragon . . . some scaly creature with many heads, perhaps, that feeds upon young maidens once they are fattened. No wonder he feeds you so well."

"Yes," said the eldest. "The better you feed, the better he will later."

"Poor child — how can we save her?"

"We cannot save her. He's too powerful, this monster. She must save herself."

"I won't listen to another word!" cried Psyche, leaping up. "You are wicked evil-minded shrews, both of you! I'm ashamed of you. Ashamed of myself for listening to you. I never want to see you again. Never!"

She struck a gong. The table was snatched away. A window flew open and the west wind swept in, curled his arm about the two sisters, swept them out and back to their own homes. Psyche was left alone, frightened, bitterly unhappy, longing for her husband. But there were still many hours till nightfall. All that long hideous afternoon she brooded about what her sisters had said. The words stuck in her mind like poison thorns. They festered in her head, throwing her into a fever of doubt.

She knew her husband was good. She knew he was beautiful. But still — why would he not let her see him? What did he do during the day? Other words of her sisters came back to her:

"How do you know what he does when he's not here? Perhaps he has dozens of castles scattered about the countryside, a princess in each one. Perhaps he visits them all."

And then jealousy, more terrible than fear, began to gnaw at her. She was not really afraid that he was a monster. Nor was she at all afraid of being devoured. If he did not love her she wanted to die anyway, but the idea that he might have other brides, other castles, clawed at her, and sent her almost mad. She felt that if she could only see him her doubts would be resolved.

As dusk began to fill the room, she took a lamp, trimmed the wick and poured in the oil. Then she lighted it, and put it in a niche of the wall where its light could not be seen. She sat down and awaited her husband.

Late that night, when he had fallen asleep, she crept away and took the torch. She tiptoed back to where he slept and held the lamp over him. There in the dim wavering light she saw a god sleeping. Eros himself, the archer of love, youngest and most beautiful of the gods. He wore a quiver of silver darts even as he slept. Her heart sang at the sight of his beauty. She leaned over to kiss his face, still holding the lamp, and a drop of hot oil fell on his bare shoulder.

He started up and seized the lamp, and doused its light. She reached for him, felt him push her away. She heard his voice saying, "Wretched girl — you are not ready to accept love. Yes, I am love itself, and I cannot live where I am not believed. Farewell, Psyche."

The voice was gone. She rushed into the courtyard, calling after him, calling, "Husband! Husband!" She heard a dry cracking sound, and when she looked back the castle was gone too. The courtyard was gone. Everything was gone. She stood among weeds and brambles. All the good things that had belonged to her vanished with her love.

From that night on, she roamed the woods, searching. And some say she still searches the woods and the dark places. Some say that Aphrodite turned her into an owl who sees best in the dark, and cries, "Who . . .? Who . . .?"

Others say she was turned into a bat that haunts old ruins, and sees only by night.

Others say her husband forgave her, finally; that he came back for her, and took her up to Olympus, where she helps him with his work of making young love. It is her special task, they say, to undo the talk of the bride's family, and the groom's. When mother or sister visit bride or groom and say, "This, this, this . . . that, that, that . . . better look for yourself; seeing's believing, seeing's believing," then she calls the west wind, who whips them away, and she, herself, invisible, whispers to them that none but love knows the secret of love, that believing is seeing.

Wise men of science have now decided that certain animals may be able to speak, and have begun to study dolphins to find out if this is true.

The old stories are full of clever beasts. Talking is the least they did. The dolphin, in particular, frisks through the blue waters of mythology. There is something about this playful fish which has always tickled the fancy of those who tell stories. So the scientists are actually in good company.

There is the story of Arion. He was the son of Poseidon and a naiad, and favored by Apollo, who taught him to play the lyre most beautifully. Arion lived in Corinth. He was a brave adventurous young man, and wanted very much to travel. But an oracle had said, "No ship will bring you back from any voyage you make."

So he was forced to stay at home. For his twentieth birthday Apollo gave him a golden lyre, and he was wild to try it out at music festivals held in Sicily and Italy.

"Oracles are gloomy by nature," he said to himself. "It is rare you hear of a happy prophecy. Besides, I must see the world no matter what happens."

Thereupon he took his lyre and set sail for Italy. He competed in the festival at Tarentum, and won all the prizes. He played and sang so beautifully that the audience was mad with delight, and heaped gifts upon him: a jeweled sword, a suit of silver armor, an ivory bow and a quiver of bronze-tipped arrows. He was so happy and triumphant that he forgot all about the prophecy, and took the first ship back to Corinth, although the captain was a huge, ugly, dangerous-looking fellow, with an even uglier crew.

On the first afternoon out, Arion was sitting in the bow, gazing at the purple sea and absently fingering his lyre, when the captain strode up, and said, "Pity . . . you're young to die."

"Am I to die young?" said Arion.

"Yes."

"How do you know?"

"Because I'm going to kill you."

"That does seem a pity," said Arion. "When is this sad event to take place?"

"Soon; in fact, immediately."

"But why? What have I done?"

"Something foolish. Permitted yourself to become the owner of a treasure which I must have. That jeweled sword, that silver armor — you should never show things like that to thieves."

"Why don't you take what you want without killing me?"

"No. We thought it over, and decided it would be safer to kill you. It usually is in these cases. Then the person who's been robbed can't complain, you see. It makes it safer for us."

"Well, I see you've thought the matter over carefully," said Arion. "So I have nothing more to say. One favor, though: Let me sing a last song before I die."

At the music festival Arion had invented a song of praise, called the dithyramb. He sang one now — praising first Apollo who had taught him music, and then his father, Poseidon, master of the sea. Then he sang a song of praise to the sea itself and all who dwell there — the naiads and Nereids and gliding fishes. He sang to the magical change-fulness of these waters which put on different colors as the sun climbs and sinks, silver and amethyst in the early light, hot blue at noon, smoky purple at dusk. He sang to the sea, smiling, treacherously kind, offering the gift of cool death for any hot grief.

So singing, he leaped from the bow of the vessel, lyre in hand, and plunged into the sea.

He had sung so beautifully that the creatures of the deep had risen to hear him. His most eager listeners were a school of dolphins, who love music. The largest dolphin dived under him, and rose to the surface lifting Arion on his back.

"Thank you, friend," said Arion.

"A poor favor to return for such heavenly music," said the dolphin.

The dolphin swam away with Arion on his back, the other dolphins frisking about, dancing on the water, as Arion played. They swam very swiftly, and Arion arrived at Taenarus and made his way to Corinth a day before the ship was due. He went immediately to the palace, to his friend, Periander, King of Corinth, and told him his story. Then he took the king down to the waterfront to introduce him to the dolphin. The fish, who had become very fond of Arion, longed to stay with him at the court of Periander, and when he died soon after, Arion gave him a magnificent funeral.

The next day the ship arrived in port. Captain and crew were seized by the king's guard, and taken to the castle. Arion stayed hidden.

"Why have you taken us captive, O king?" said the captain. "We are peaceable law-abiding sailors."

"My friend Arion took passage on your ship!" roared the king. "Where is he? What have you done with him?"

"Poor lad," said the captain. "He was quite mad. He was on deck singing to himself one day, and then suddenly jumped overboard. We put out a small boat, circled the spot for hours. We couldn't find a trace. Sharks, probably. The sea's full of them there."

"And what do you sailors do to a man-eating shark when you catch him?" asked the king.

"Kill him, of course," said the captain. "Can't let them swim free and endanger other sailors."

"A noble sentiment," said Arion, stepping out of his hiding place. "And that's exactly what we do to two-legged sharks in Corinth."

So captain and crew were taken out and hanged. The

ship was searched, and Arion's property restored to him. He insisted on dividing the rich gifts with the king. When Periander protested, Arion laughed, and said, "Treasures are trouble. You're a king and can handle them. But I am a minstrel. I must travel light."

And all his life he sang songs of praise. His music grew in power and beauty until people said he was a second Orpheus. When he died, Apollo set him in the sky, him and his lyre and the dolphin too. And they shine in the night sky still, the stars of the constellation Arion. They shine on pirates and minstrels, on wise men trying to learn the language of animals, and on simple men who have always known it.

# AFTERWORD

Greek mythology has inspired almost every person who has come into contact with its countless delights and bewitching magic. Because these ancient stories are so exciting and present interpretations of some natural phenomena, they are constantly cropping up in various forms today. We see them in modern plays, novels, television programs, movies, and even in advertisements.

In the past, primitive men created their own imaginative explanations for things they could not understand. They heard an echo as another voice responding from the heavens. They believed the changing of the seasons, the rising and setting of the sun, and many other natural effects from natural causes were really the results of the persistent, intense will of the gods. Primitive men had no geologists to tell them that the earth had slowly evolved over millions of years, so they invented their own explanations of creation and of the origins of life and death. Even in our modern scientific age, we cannot explain all natural phenomena, but we assume they have been or will be explained by someone who has more information and understanding than we have. We do not try to make our own interpretations.

Primitive man was always asking questions and trying to find answers; he was challenged by the unknown, and since there were no established laws of science, no acknowledged authorities, he found for himself magnificent answers in the form of stories. The collective imaginations of the Greeks became the mythology we have today.

This mythology has significance for several reasons. It has been kept alive long after the culture in which it evolved has disappeared. If we want to trace our own heritage back to the past, mythology offers an excellent way of doing it. Mythology was a religion to the Greeks as well as being their literature and philosophy; consequently, it provides an excellent demonstration of their ideas, modes of life, and the nature of their civilization. To understand the myths is to understand the people who created them and to understand their way of life, so different from our own. To be familiar with the gods who inhabited Greek Olympus is to perceive the meaning and the spirit of literature, art, and music of ancient times.

The myths also manifest themselves surprisingly in myriad ways in our modern world, in the names of some of the days of the week, months of the year, names of planets, names of spaceships and rockets, and above all, in words we use every day in our conversation.

Of course, in addition to the ways they illuminate ancient life, the myths have a fascination in, and of, themselves; they are exciting stories full of beauty, strangeness, power, freshness, and adventure.

The Greeks, we are told, came from tribes from the south-central part of Asia who came to the land now known as Greece about 2000 B.C. At first these tribes settled in the valleys or in the hills or along the seacoast. They were very proud of their particular settlements. Each group created its own individual myths or stories and thus the myths reflect the place of their origin. Gradually, however, these individual groups merged and in time the Greek world included the many Aegean Islands, part of the mainland of Asia Minor as well as the peninsula of Greece. Greek myths then became a fusion of all these diverse cultures.

The Greeks accepted the idea that there were many gods and that they were very near. The gods had magnificent powers and talents, but they were eager to associate with mortals. In many ways the myths also reveal typically human characteristics. To the early Greeks, life was something to enjoy, to take delight in, and to inspire one with awe. They were aware of the presence of mystery in everything; they responded to compelling beauty in nature and people.

There are almost as many forms of the myths as there are people who tell them, but each variation has elements in common. We hope the Greek myths in this book have helped to bring the fascinating world of the Greeks closer to you.

# WORD ORIGINS

A great many words we use today are derived from Greek myths. It is interesting to trace the origin of some of these words and to see how we have adapted them for our own use.

**Arachne,** meaning "spider" in Greek, was adopted to describe in science the spider family which includes scorpions, mites, and ticks: arachnida or arachnoidea. The adjective *arachnoid* means anything resembling a spider's web.

**Athene** was also known as Pallas Athene. Pallas signifies "brandisher," that is, as a spear. An asteroid was named Pallas as well as a very rare metallic element called palladium which was named after the asteroid. Because a statue of Pallas Athene which stood in front of the city of Troy was supposed to have helped preserve the city from danger, the word *palladium* also has come to mean a potent safeguard.

**Calliope** is the name of a musical instrument. The mother of Orpheus was named Calliope because she was the Muse of Eloquence and Heroic Poetry. The name comes from two words meaning "beauty" and "voice."

**Cronos** refers to the god of time. From this word we have the noun *chronology* which describes an arrangement of events in order of occurrence. *Chronic* describes something that continues over a long period of time. A chronicler is one who records a historical account of events in the order of time. A timepiece of great accuracy is called a chronometer.

**Cyclops,** plural **Cyclopes,** is derived from two Greek words meaning "circle" and "eye." We have adopted *cyclops* in the field of biology to describe the group of tiny, free-swimming crustaceans which have a single eye. *Cyclopie* is an adjective meaning monstrous; *cyclopia* is a noun used for a massive abnormality in which the eyes are partly or wholly fused. The word has been used as a root to describe a wheel in such words as tricycle, bicycle, and motorcycle. It is used to describe a violent storm which moves in a circle: cyclone. It also appears in the word encyclopedia to describe circular (or complete) learning. A cyclotron is a large apparatus used for the multiple acceleration of ions to very high speeds.

**Elysian Fields,** which means a "place of great happiness," inspired the French to call their famous boulevard in Paris the Champs Elysées.

**Erinyes,** or the Furies, punished people for their crimes on the earth. They were called the Eumenides, which meant "the kindly ones." This name reveals the Greek habit of calling unpleasant things by pleasant names. We use the word euphemism to describe words which do not say the unpleasant idea intended.

**Hades** is used today to describe the home of the dead. Hades comes from the Greek word meaning "the unseen." Hades was also known in Roman mythology as Pluto, the god of wealth—from the Greek word *plutus*, meaning "wealth." We use the word *plutocracy* to describe a government run by wealthy people.

**Jove,** one of the names for Jupiter and Zeus, has come to mean "born under a lucky planet and therefore happy and healthy." The adjective *jovial*, and the noun *jovialness* all derive from the word *Jove*. We even hear the expression, "By Jove." The planet Jupiter is the largest body in the solar system except the sun.

**Muses** refers to the nine goddesses of dancing, poetry and astronomy. We use the verb *muse* to describe the act of pondering or meditating. The words music, musician and musical all come from this word.

**Narcissus** is the name of a family of flowers which includes daffodils and jonquils. The word *narcissist* is a psychological term meaning a person who loves himself.

**Olympus** was the home of the Greek gods. The term has come to mean something which is grand, imposing, or heavenly. The great festival of games was called Olympian Games and today we call the word-famous athletic contest the Olympics.

**Oracle** is derived from the Greek word meaning "to pray." It is used to refer to places where people pray: oratories; to great speakers: orators; and even great speeches: orations. A person who seems to possess great knowledge or intuition is called an oracle, and his statements are described as oracular.

**Pandora** has the same prefix as Pantheon and means, of course, all. The root *doron* is a Greek word for gift; therefore, Pandora was all-gifted.

**Pantheon** is made up of two Greek words: *pan* meaning "all," and *theos* meaning "god," or "having something to do with gods."

The prefix *pan* is used in such words as panacea, Panama, and even Pan American. The root *theos* is used in such words as theology and theocracy.

**Prometheus** means "forethinker." It has come to mean something that is life-giving, daringly original, or creative. An element which is a fission product of uranium is called promethium. The prefix *pro* is used in countless words today.

**Python,** which comes from the Greek word "to rot," is used to describe snakes such as the boa which kills its prey by crushing it. The adjective *pythogenic* is used to describe something which is produced by putrefaction or filth.

**Stygian** comes from the river Styx. It has come to be used when describing anything from the underworld. Stygian darkness is a favorite expression of poets.

**Titan,** which referred to the race of giants, has been used to describe anything which is enormous in size or strength. The famous ship which sank when it hit an iceberg was called the *Titanic*.

# BIBLIOGRAPHY

Asimov, Isaac. *Words from the Myths*. Houghton Mifflin: Boston, 1961.

Bulfinch, Thomas. *Bulfinch's Mythology*. Thomas Y. Crowell: New York (no date).

Grant, Michael. *Myths of the Greeks and Romans*. World Publishers: New York, 1962.

Graves, Robert. *The Greek Myths*. Penguin Books: Baltimore, 1955.

Hamilton, Edith. *Mythology*. New American Library: New York, 1940.

Hamilton, Edith. *The Greek Way to Western Civilization*. New American Library: New York, 1948.

Hays, H. R. *In The Beginnings*. G. P. Putnam's Sons: New York, 1963.

Rose, H. J. *A Handbook of Greek Mythology*. E. P. Dutton: New York, 1959.

Schwab, Gustav. *Gods and Heroes: Myths and Epics of Ancient Greece*. Fawcett World Library: New York, 1965.

Updike, John. *The Centaur*. Knopf: New York, 1963.